KGB & SOVIET SECURITY UNIFORMS & MILITARIA
1917-1991
IN COLOUR PHOTOGRAPHS

KGB & SOVIET SECURITY UNIFORMS & MILITARIA

1917-1991

IN COLOUR PHOTOGRAPHS

Committee for State Security and
Ministry of Internal Affairs of the USSR:
Militia, Internal Forces, Spetznaz, Frontier Guards, etc.

LÁSZLÓ BÉKÉSI

Photographs by

GYÖRGY TÖRÖK

The Crowood Press

First published in 2002 by
The Crowood Press Ltd
Ramsbury, Marlborough
Wiltshire SN8 2HR

© László Békési 2002
Photographs © György Török 2002

Dedication
This book is dedicated to every
citizen of the former Soviet Union
throughout its 74-year history.

Edited by Martin Windrow
Design by Frank Ainscough
@ Compendium

Printed in Singapore by
Craft Print International

Colour origination by
Black Cat Graphics Ltd,
Bristol, England

British Library
Cataloguing-in-Publication Data
A CIP catalogue record for this book
is available from the British Library

ISBN 1 86126 511 5

Contents

Preface

I started to collect Soviet uniforms and militaria in 1987, when I was 17 years old. It was not a popular hobby in Budapest, where, unsurprisingly, a stereotyped image of the Soviet Army lived on in most peoples' minds. In 1990 I went on a summer student exchange to the Leningrad Institute of Finance, named after Voznesensky, the academic planner of the World War II military economy. In Budapest we were already studying Western-style economics, and most students wanted to go to Western universities - mine was the last Hungarian student group ever to go to the USSR. After a 'white night' in Leningrad, when I spent hours in the square of the Winter Palace - scene of one of the great mythic moments of the 1917 Revolution - I went back to my student dormitory in the early hours. A policeman was guarding the entrance; I had no passport or entry card with me.

I had talked often with Soviet soldiers in Hungary, but this was different: he was a Soviet policeman, a symbol of the Communist state security machine. Sadly for the theatrical requirements of the stereotype, he did not want to beat me up, put me in jail, listen in to my telephone conversations, or even to cut my very long hair. Actually he was a grandfather, and we had a pleasant chat; I still remember his name. (So I missed out on the advantages which some people nowadays have built on somewhat shaky claims to have been victims of Soviet power.)

It was then that I decided that I would like to pursue my interest in a subject which was hardly fashionable. Over the years which have followed I have set up a collection of Soviet armed forces uniforms, equipment, insignia and awards. To have any interest from a scholarly point of view this collection has necessarily been supported by the assembly of additional archives - thousands of original photographs, documents, and all related regulations, books, articles and periodicals. I have also amassed useful information, and invaluable 'hands-on experience', during my journeys to visit libraries, museums and archives, and many meetings with historians, experts and other collectors.

It has been a hobby which has led to a number of encounters, in the former USSR and in other countries, with people who sometimes found my motives perplexing. The librarians of the military archives in St Petersburg were somewhat taken aback to be visited by a foreigner who knew exactly what he wanted, asked specific questions, and already knew most of the books they brought out for him. There was some discussion in Kiev about a Hungarian who bought dozens of Soviet naval daggers. At Huizen, near Amsterdam, Holland, it was not felt particularly unusual that a boy from the East should enter and win a chess competition, but his parallel activities of buying and selling Soviet uniforms and badges caused some questions. The officers in a high security Spanish police station at San Sebastian in the Basque country were at first baffled when a Hungarian student walked in, but in the end some of them returned to the station from their homes to see and exchange his police arm patches, and they did not finish talking until late into the night. In 1992 an old Russian lady turned up in a small square near Budapest, because she had heard in Moscow that there was a boy there who was interested in buying an Order of Lenin.

I was once questioned by plain clothes agents in a police car in the Cairo bazaar because I had been overheard haggling over Egyptian camouflage uniforms and paratrooper badges. On another occasion I bought 4,000 caps from the Hungarian Ministry of Internal Affairs when the police replaced their former Socialist uniforms. A lady language teacher at the Hungarian Police Academy became so irritated with a civilian student taking a Russian internal affairs language exam that she ejected him, for insisting on the correct terms for various KGB border patrol boat flags - names which she had never heard. I was not discouraged: as a student at an economic geography seminar, I drew up as a representative exercise a 'World Map of the Prices of Soviet Peaked Caps'. It is remarkable where an adolescent interest in old badges can lead you.

AUTHOR'S NOTE

This book is the second in what I hope will become a series, offering visual images of uniforms and militaria from a wide sweep of Soviet military history. The first, published in 2000 and entitled *Soviet Uniforms and Militaria 1917-1991 in Colour Photographs,* is devoted to forces under the control of the Ministry of Defence of the USSR - the Army, Navy ('Fleet'), and Air Force (including airborne troops). It contains a good deal of general information on Soviet uniform and insignia practice, of equal relevance to some services covered in the present volume; to avoid too much duplication, cross-references to it will be found in the pages which follow, in the form *Book 1.*

I have tried to give both the Russian names and acronyms of the various major organisations covered in this book, with reasonably close English translations. For consistency I have chosen the term Ministry of Internal Affairs for the MVD, Frontier Guards for the PV, and Internal Forces for the VV. The term Militia should be understood to mean the various Police forces in all contexts.

Naming exact colours is always difficult, since over a period of 70 years of dispersed manufacture neither regulation nor vernacular terms match up with the actual perceived colours with any consistency. For instance, 'cornflower' blue has varied in practice between a very dark, almost 'navy' blue and quite a bright 'royal' shade. Throughout, I have used the description 'raspberry' red for the crimson shade used to distinguish, *inter alia*, the infantry branch of the Red Army; and 'brick' red for the duller shade used for Internal Forces distinctions, though this has varied between a true orange-red and simply a dull maroon. In all instances it is our hope that the colour photographs of actual items will resolve any confusion. On another point of usage, I have used the American term 'visored cap' throughout, rather than the British 'peaked cap'.

I am currently working on another project focusing purely on World War II, especially the combat uniforms and militaria of 'Stalin's War'. Since the publication of *Soviet Uniforms and Militaria 1917-1991* I have received increasing numbers of letters and e-mails with orders, questions, and shared information from private collectors, professional archivists and film industry contacts alike - from countries as diverse as the UK and Ireland, France, Italy, Portugal, the Netherlands, the USA, Canada, Australia, Japan (where at the January 2002 Tokyo Military Show a small fight broke out over the last copy on the author's stand), and Hong Kong, as well as the former USSR and Warsaw Pact nations. It is my hope that this second book will encourage this flow of contacts further - my addresses are given on the dust-jacket flap.

ACKNOWLEDGEMENTS

I would like to thank all the individuals and institutions who gave me information, material and time during the preparation of this book, especially: Ministry of Defence of the Hungarian Republic, Press Department; and the former Danube Flotilla. The librarians, archivists and research fellows of the following Russian institutions, all in St Petersburg: University of MVD of the Russian Federation, especially Ida Semyonovna; Military-Historical Museum of Artillery, Engineers and Signals, especially Sergei Anatolievich Lazarev, senior research fellow; Central Archives of the Navy. The OTKA 34265/F30362 Research Project; Tibor Pirisi, Györgyi and Szilárd Szócska, the late Gyula Jászberényi - a great photographer, who died at an early stage of this work; Min Fan-chiang, Davide Samueli, Valentina and Sveta Tchentsova, Ella and Igor, István Kiss, Tamás Kiss, Igor Tziganov, Ibolya and Jura, Alex, Alek, Vasya, Leonid, and Alyosha. Particular thanks for the patience of our models, Éva Bánhidi, Mónika Nyul, Balázs Jásdi, Ferenc Rippel, Sergei Semyonov Naumovich, Konstantin Titkov Viktorovich, Zoltán Vass and Erzsébet Schlegl.

The inspiration for this work came from the published researches of Andrew Mollo; his book was the first on modern uniforms that I ever read, ten years ago on the beach of the Lido, Venice, while everybody else was swimming.

Introduction

This book deals with the uniforms, insignia, some personal equipment and memorabilia of the Soviet state security and law enforcement agencies. Their history and evolution as organisations was more complex than that of the Red Army or the other armed forces controlled by the Ministry of Defence of the USSR. To those with the eyes to see, their uniforms and insignia offer clues to the great historical cycles of modernity and historicism, patriotism and Communist internationalism, following the tone of contemporary propaganda. These cycles were governed by changes in Soviet geopolitical and strategic power relations, and in the international (and sometimes domestic) balance of powers.

The whole 70-year period saw successive structural changes in the organisation of the Soviet state's security machine, from the first days of the 1917 October Revolution; in fact, even before the Revolution there were theoretical debates about the role of police and security forces in the new, modern, revolutionary Russian state whose creation had long been planned. The centre of interest often moved, as the Communist state focused on and created new enemies and target groups. The security organisations were loosed on the trail of various real or imagined anti-revolutionary classes and forces: at first, against such obvious former supporters of the Tsarist regime as aristocrats, entrepreneurs (i.e. anyone who bought and sold), and Imperial military and administrative personnel. Later their baleful eyes were turned on intellectuals, artists, peasants who stood in the way of collectivisation, ethnic minorities, the religious, and foreign capitalists; later still the Stalinist terror would consume Russian and foreign Communists, including many veteran Bolsheviks. Practically between one day and the next, any and every identifiable individual or group could become the 'enemy of the workers' - even stamp collectors. As late as the time of President Gorbachev in the 1980s, heavy drinkers were targeted as a distinct, anti-social group.

The agencies of state security were also involved in - or helped to create - the international conflicts of the 20th century. The VTchK or 'Cheka' headed by Felix Dzerzhinsky played a most active role in the Civil War which immediately followed the Revolution. The Frontier Guards, which came under the command of the NKVD, were the first armed units to try to resist the German invasion from the first hours of Operation Barbarossa in June 1941 - and would be fighting Afghan 'counter-revolutionaries' 40 years later. During the 'Great Patriotic War' of 1941-45 NKVD troops, while seldom committed to front line combat against the Germans, were prominent immediately behind the lines in enforcing total dedication to the war effort. During the Cold War, KGB and other state security personnel were sent all over the world to support Communist movements; they planned the taking over of power - or, once it had been seized, they defended it, as in Hungary in 1956 and Czechoslovakia in 1968. Amongst other military and strategic advisers they played their part in the turmoils of the Third World, for instance in Cuba, Angola, Mozambique, Egypt and Nicaragua.

The organisation of this book follows the structure of our previous title *Soviet Uniforms and Militaria 1917-1991 in Colour Photographs*. It is divided chronologically, into relatively short initial sections on the pre-war and World War II security forces, and a much more substantial section on the state security and internal organisations of the Cold War period.

At the end of the book will be found material on various unarmed but uniformed organisations under the control of other ministries. We hope that this will be helpful for comparative purposes of identification. The USSR had a vast range of uniformed services, and photographs, uniform items and insignia have often been misidentified to the military or security services. Indeed, collectors excited by some previously unseen find have even tried to create 'back-stories' about unknown or secret armed forces units in order to identify a cap or badge which may in reality have belonged to a railway worker, an ambulance driver, a merchant sailor or a postman.

SELECT BIBLIOGRAPHY & FURTHER READING
In English:
László Békési, *Soviet Uniforms and Militaria 1917-1991 in Colour Photographs*, The Crowood Press, Ramsbury, 2000
László Békési, 'The Return of Tsarist Symbols in the Great Patriotic War', Sociology PhD dissertation
M.Degtyarev, V.Krylov, & A.Kulinsky, *The Weapons of Kalashnikov*, exhibition catalogue, The Artillery Museum, St Petersburg, no date
V.A.Durov, *Russian and Soviet Military Awards*, Order of Lenin State History Museum, 1990
I.I.Likhitskiy: *Art of Russian Miniature*, badge catalogue, Udacha, Lvov, 1995
Andrew Mollo, *The Armed Forces of World War II*, Orbis, London, 1981
Gregori Alexandrovich Putnikov, *Orders and Medals of the USSR*, Novosti, Moscow, 1990

A.Shalito, I.Savchenkov & Andew Mollo, *Red Army Uniforms of World War II*, (Europa Militaria Series No.14), Windrow and Geene, London, 1993
I.Tokar, *History of Russian Uniform: Soviet Police 1918-1991*, Exclusive Publishing House, St Petersburg, 1995
In Russian:
V.D.Krivtzov: *Variations (Collectors' Guide)*, Vols 1-5, Moscow, 1995-2001
Anatoliy Nikolaevich Kutzenko, *Cap Badges of Ministries and Authorities of the USSR*, Aspect, Slovenian Republic, 1998
Anatoliy Nikolaevich Kutzenko, *Awards of the Law Enforcement Organs of the USSR*, Donetsk, 1991
N.V.Ogarkov (ed.), *Soviet Military Encyclopedia*, Vols 1-8, Ministry of Defence, Moscow, 1980
Your Military Uniform, Political Directorate of the Headquarters of the Internal Forces of the MVD, Moscow, 1986
A.B.Zhuk, *Handbook of Firearms*, Voyenizdat, Moscow, 1993

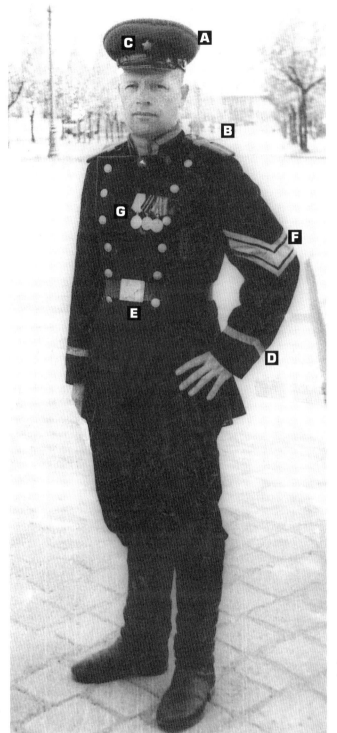

Traffic Police Sergeant-Major, 1948. *This photograph offers a good exercise in 'decoding' a picture of a Soviet serviceman, to identify his service, rank and date when we lack any precise caption. We show here a relatively straightforward example; the detective work may sometimes be more complex – for instance when KGB, PV or VV insignia have been applied to various uniforms of the Ministry of Defence services.*

First, the service: the dark colour of the uniform marks him as a Militiaman - a police officer, uniformed in dark blue or black. We can see that the crown of the visored cap (**A**) *is of a medium shade, with a darker band. The combination of red top and black band would be typical for Traffic Police personnel, who wore black uniforms. To be certain, we have to exclude other services which wore red-crowned caps. These were indeed worn by some cavalry troopers in the 1920s; but this picture is definitely not from the 1920s, because the shoulderboards* (**B**) *must date from 1943 at the earliest, when these adornments were restored for the first time since the Revolution. The buckle plate also points to a date well after the 1920s. Railway personnel also wore red-topped caps, but with the badge of a crossed hammer and monkey wrench; this man wears a star badge* (**C**). *So he is neither a cavalryman nor a railway worker. This cap was in use from 1943; the red top had blue piping. In this period other types of Militia units wore a cap badge comprising the coat of arms of the USSR; but our man wears the Army-style star, used only by Traffic and Waterways Police.*

Another clue to the Traffic Police is the yellow inverted chevron passing

right around his cuffs (**D**) *- in fact this had red piping along the top, though it is invisible in this monochrome photograph. The Army-style belt buckle* (**E**) *was commonly worn by transport police enlisted ranks; in fact, this picture is one of the first pieces of evidence that Militiamen received this buckle before it became Army general issue in 1951 (it has been speculated that Army cadets had already begun receiving it after 1943). The buckle is first mentioned in Militia regulations for 1947.*

Rank is not a problem. His shoulderboards clearly display a broad lengthways stripe and a transverse stripe making a T-shape - unmistakably the sign of a sergeant-major. The sleeve chevrons (**F**) *just above the elbow were worn - though not often - to mark long service, between 1945 and 1952. He has one golden yellow above two silver, marking the third year of his professional Militia service. Under magnification we can identify his medals* (**G**), *for Military Merit, Victory over Germany, and the 30th Anniversary of the Armed Forces - which fell in 1948. So the date of the photograph is not before 1948, but not later than 1952.*

Most probably it was taken in 1948: he is clearly in parade dress order, in a piped, double-breasted tunic with a braided stand collar. Yet a new single-breasted tunic was introduced for parade wear in 1947; thus 1948 was probably the latest date when our man would have worn his old M1943 double-breasted tunic. We may guess that the photograph was taken on either May Day 1948, or VE-Day, a week later on 8 May.

THE EARLY YEARS, 1917-41
The Workers' and Peasants' Militia

To distinguish the security forces of the new Revolutionary state from the hated Imperial police or *Politia*, the forces of public order were named *Militia* - originally, the Workers' and Peasants' Militia (RKM), just as the army was initially titled the Workers' and Peasants' Red Army (RKKA). The police services retained the title Militia throughout the history of the Soviet Union.

In the aftermath of the Revolution all former state institutions and organisations were abolished, reshaped and/or renamed. For instance, until the end of World War II there were no 'Ministries'; throughout the USSR power was exercised through Committees, Commissariats, Secretariats and Colleges, and this included the organs of state security. It was the fashion to use abbreviations or acronyms when referring to the new organisations, and to groups supportive of, or even hostile to the Revolution. For instance, during the 1920s a separate department of the '*Cheka*' was tasked with fighting against 'the NEPers': this meant that one of the departments of the VTchK, the All-Russian Extraordinary Commission for Struggle against Counter-Revolution and Sabotage (the actual name of the central state security organisation), was dedicated to combating the activities of black marketeers. These illicit traders were ironically named after the abbreviation of the 'New Economic Policy' or NEP introduced by Lenin after the catastrophic failure of the early Revolutiontary experiments; this revived some elements of a market economy - such as money.

The lavish use of acronyms persisted throughout the life of the Soviet Union, and in the chapters which follow will be found brief explanations of such often confusing usages as VTchK, (O)GPU, NKVD, MGB, MVD, KGB, VV, PV, OMON and SPETZNAZ.

MILITIAMEN, 1918 AND EARLY 1920s.

(Opposite) Militiaman, 1918. He wears a superior quality gymnastiorka - the traditional Russian pullover shirt-tunic - with pleated patch pockets and piped patches on the tight fall collar; the latter bear buttons but no rank insignia. The cap has a small, soft leather down-turned peak which is more decorative than functional; it bears a small red shield-shaped badge. His Nagant revolver is carried butt forwards on his right hip in a non-regulation pre-Revolutionary holster, with a lanyard to the belt. Note his spurred boots - spurs were often also sported by non-mounted police, although the other photograph of this same man (right) shows him mounted.

MILITIA COMMANDER, 1924

Grey and blue were the distinctive colours of Militia uniforms throughout the Soviet period. This chief of a town's police department wears everyday working uniform, with only one left breast pocket; because of shortages of parade and walking-out dress he would wear the same uniform for parades on national holidays, etc., with the addition of knee boots and his Red Star Order decoration. His revolver holster hangs from a shoulder belt independently from the waist belt, the latter having a one-prong open frame buckle. He also carries a small black case for documents such as town maps, likewise slung separate from the waist belt.

(Above) M1924 NKVD collar patches. Note the shape and the colours; the buttons are the same as Army issue.

(Right) Militia breast badge. This was introduced in March 1923 by Order No.180 of the NKVD - Narodny Kommissariat Vnutrennikh Del, *People's Commissariat for Internal Affairs,* the new name for the national state security agency, with overall control of the police forces. The upper wreathed shield motif was repeated in the Militia cap badge; note that the additional lower plaque of the breast badge was individually numbered. To avoid any confusion over the identity of policemen, no other badge, medal or order was to be worn with it except on occasions of state or political ceremony. Note, beneath the badge, a strengthened hole for the attachment of the pin-on Red Star Order for such parade occasions.

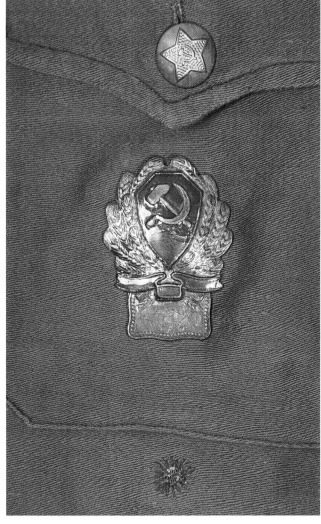

MEDIUM COMMANDER, NKVD CRIMINAL INVESTIGATION SERVICE, 1928

As in the Red Army, formal officers' rank titles had been replaced by various categories of 'commander'. This inspector wears everyday summer uniform, his department identified by the green-piped collar patches. Note his high quality boots and professional camera.

(Above) **The gymnastiorka.** *The buttons bear the coat of arms of the Soviet Union. The only badge or decoration allowed to be worn was the Red Star Order, illustrated here. After 1925 and until 1928 ranks were identified on the collar patches (as in the Red Army) by red-enamelled geometric forms - triangles, squares, bars and diamonds. At the end of 1928 these were replaced by different numbers of differently coloured shield shapes; but in 1931 the NKVD reverted to the geometric forms as rank indicators. The green piping was displayed only by criminal investigators.*

(Right) **Collar emblem.** *The shield motif was always prominent in the symbolism of the state security agencies - NKVD, MVD and KGB units - at every period of Soviet history.*

(Above) Workers' and Peasants' Militia, Ukraine, 1930. Although various black coats were introduced for the Militia under the 1923 regulations, most of these policemen wear standard grey Army coats and fleece papaha winter hats. Under magnification the second man from left in the front complete row can be seen to wear the Militia breast badge and cap badge. The young cadet in the centre of this group wears a regulation black coat. In the pre-war period, especially before the 1930s, a variety of irregular uniforms and insignia might be seen in some territories due both to different climatic conditions (e.g. in the warmer Far East, Crimea, or Asian Soviet Republics), and to local unavailability of materials or facilities (especially in the Ukraine, which suffered from a disastrous famine).

(Left) Militia Cadet, 1934. There were separate training schools for the equivalents of officers and non-commissioned officers, although the best graduates from the latter might proceed to the former. The collar patches were blue with red piping and gold Cyrillic characters. Cadets of the senior command schools displayed three characters (here the 'TzVSh' probably stands for Central High School); the schools for 'medium' personnel had two characters, the initial of the location (e.g. 'L' for Leningrad) followed by 'Sh' for school. Note the shoulder brace of his M1932 belt system. This is the same man as illustrated on page 9, and in three of the photographs opposite.

(Above left and right) 4th Category Militiaman, winter and summer uniforms, 1931. This rank, identified by two red-enamelled squares on the collar patch, was one of those introduced by the reforms of 1931, the former titles being replaced by a simple sequence which was used until 1936: militiaman, first category militiaman, second category militiaman, and so on up to thirteenth category (who was the chief of the central police agency).

In both of these pictures he wears the same grey-topped cap with red band and piping but, irregularly, without chin strap and side buttons. Another irregularity is the cap

badge: from 1931 the shield-shaped red badge shown here was officially replaced by a blue star. This kind of non-regulation uniform detail or incomplete change was usual in small, remote rural stations manned by only a few policemen, who might simply have no acess to the new items. Note that the top of the hat is not stiffened flat; he has set it up with two small 'valleys' at the front of the crown. Usually the white summer gymnastiorka was worn with a white cap or a white 'helmet cap' similar to the British 'bobby's' helmet. Note his sapagi knee boots in the summer photograph; and the cut of the winter coat cuffs, rising steeply to a point at the rear.

(Left) Militia Commander Candidate, 1936. Note the stripes on the collar patches, which do not bear stars of rank. Trainee commanders, e.g. inspector or squad leader, were called candidates at this stage. Note that the cap badge was so large that the chin strap had to be fitted behind its lower edge. See an NKVD commander from the same year with similar collar stripes on page 16.

(Left) Junior Lieutenant of Militia, Crimea, 1939. Note the metal coat of arms badge just visible pinned above his left elbow - for detail, see colour photograph on page 31. On the left breast he wears one of the shooting proficiency badges of the 1920s. His belt is made for wearing a sword (note the two D-rings below the shoulder brace attachment on the left side); police did not carry rubber truncheons until the 1960s. The sharovary breeches are blue. The wide light blue M1936 collar patches of rank (see also page 16) display one gold stripe with two silver stars, one centred above and one below it. Stars were the same size for all ranks at this date; after the reforms of 1943, majors and higher ranks displayed larger stars.

NKVD - People's Commissariat
for Internal Affairs

(Right) NKVD cap, 1924. The colours of the state security service visored cap were significant from the mid-1920s until the mid-1950s. The crown is 'cornflower blue' (dark blue); the band and piping are of the same 'raspberry red' colour that distinguished the infantry branch of the Red Army. Note that before the mid-1930s the top of the cap was not worn flat; thereafter a round metal strip stiffener was inserted to keep the crown circular and flat-topped.

(Below right) NKVD budionovka cap, mid-1920s. This winter headgear was made to a high quality for career personnel; conscripts' winter equipment was sometimes designed to last for only one or two cold seasons. The very high point was not normally seen later than the early 1930s. The bone buttons fasten strong leather straps retaining the rolled flap. Note the raspberry red cloth star edged with black (officially, dark blue). Compare this cap with the later NKVD man's budionovka illustrated on page 23.

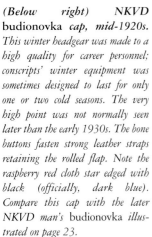

(Below left) NKVD Commander, 1936. NKVD Internal Forces and Militia adopted a new rank system in this year, marked by a sequence of insignia similar to that seen on the former Imperial shoulderboards, with various combinations of stars and stripes, but displayed on light blue collar patches. This featured combinations of a maximum of three gold stripes and four silver stars: e.g. lieutenant, two stripes and three stars; inspector, three stripes and two stars, etc. The meaning of this single stripe without stars is that the individual has already been appointed to commander's rank but has not yet completed his training or education. Promotion to higher positions depended more upon bravery, conspicuous determination and political reliability than upon education or length of service - a common feature of all revolutionary forces.

Note the bronze breast badge, also introduced in 1936, which marks his recognition as an Excellent Security Worker during the construction of the Moscow-Volga Canal. Large modernisation projects were organised and controlled by the NKVD to minimise the possibility of sabotage and technical or organisational problems, and the enforcement of strict time schedules. Such projects,

especially those related to hydro-electric schemes and electrification, were hailed as demonstrating the superiority of the Communist system. The benefits of these propaganda successes could be frustrated by shortages of materials or of manpower. Many labourers on these large scale public works were genuine volunteers, but many were forced workers - armed forces units, political prisoners, or former elites of the Imperial period condemned to hard labour as a part of their 'work therapy'. In one of the most gigantic projects Moscow was to become a port by its connection to five seas by means of canal systems, all the Moscow River bridges in the capital being heightened to allow the passage of large seagoing ships. During the 1930s many heavy industrial factories, railways, mines and power stations were constructed under NKVD control; another major state project supervised by a separate NKVD department was the system of 'Gulag' labour camps in hidden locations.

Other known NKVD badges related to this period of state modernisation projects are those for railways, mines and Far East industrialisation. Note that after World War II medals were awarded for the same kind of work activity, but without explicit State Security involvement.

LIEUTENANT-COLONEL, NKVD STATE SECURITY, 1936

As a prestigious officer of the NKVD he has a smart walking-out uniform. The fall-collar tunic has collar patches in the state security distinguishing colour of a dull brick red, although the band and piping on his cap, and seam piping on the dark blue trousers remain raspberry red. Straight-cut trousers were sometimes worn, as here, loose over shoes, for walking-out or administrative duties; on other occasions, e.g. with field or winter uniform, breeches and boots were worn. The State Security embroidered patch is sewn to both sleeves for maximum visibility. His decorations are the Red Banner Order for the Civil War period, and the Red Star Order for suffering serious wounds or injury in service. He carries in his hand a set of parade orders.

(Below) **Detail of the NKVD State Security sleeve patch, of gold and silver embroidery.** *It is sewn to the cloth of the sleeve with fine hand-stitching around the edge.*

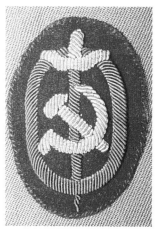

(Right) **Red Banner Orders.** *Top centre is the early type, instituted in 1918, a pin-on decoration worn without a ribbon. Between 1918 and 1924 it bore the legend 'RSFSR' (Russian Soviet Socialist Federal Republic); this was later changed to 'USSR'. The lower three* are post-1943 decorations for first, second and third awards to the same person (note the numbers at the bottom of the silver medals). Second, third, or even higher-numbered awards are extremely rare, and their price on the collectors' market is growing exponentially.

NKVD Frontier Guards

Border defence was one of the most pressing problems of the infant Soviet state, threatened by internal and external anti-Revolutionary attacks during the Civil War which persisted into the 1920s. On 28 May 1918, Lenin decreed the formation of the first regular border defence troops. Their equipment and uniform were ordered standardised from 6 September that year. From then onwards they wore the famous green-topped visored cap (and Persian lamb *papaha*), and green-based insignia; green had already been a distinction of the border troops before the Revolution.

Between 1918 and 1922 the command of the Frontier Guards and responsibility of defending the frontiers was given to various organisations and committees: the People's Committee for Finance, People's Committee of Trade, People's Committee of Military Affairs, the *Cheka*, and the Red Army. From 1922 'The Council of Labour and Defence' placed the whole border defence system in the hands of the GPU (later OGPU) - the new title for the *Cheka* adopted in that year, (*Obyediyonoroye*) *Gosudarstvennoye Politichezkoye Upravleniye*, or (United) State Political Administration. In 1934 the OGPU amalgamated with the NKVD.

YEFREITOR, FRONTIER GUARDS ARTILLERY, c.1938

(Left) Frontier Guards units were the first to be involved in any international conflict when the USSR was on the defensive. They were accordingly issued on a limited scale with heavy equipment such as artillery, armoured cars, patrol boats, and even aircraft. Two of the best-known border conflicts of the inter-war period were those triggered by the expansionist Japanese Kwangtung Army in the Far East, on the border between Manchukuo (Japanese-occupied Manchuria) and Soviet Outer Mongolia in July-August 1938, and in the Khalkyn Gol or Nomonhan campaign of May-September 1939 - the latter ending in a decisive Russian victory.

This light canvas tropical uniform is worn with a green-topped furashka *visored cap and short* batinki *boots.*

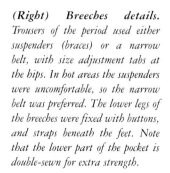

(Above) Collar details. Around the inner surface of the collar a detachable white liner was often sewn to protect the material from sweat and chafing; it was especially useful in wet or hot climates. Note that both the collar patch itself, and the metal triangle identifying yefreitor (private first class) are green for the Frontier Guards - in contrast to the rank distinctions of the Red Army and the Militia, respectively red, and blue or red.

(Right) Breeches details. Trousers of the period used either suspenders (braces) or a narrow belt, with size adjustment tabs at the hips. In hot areas the suspenders were uncomfortable, so the narrow belt was preferred. The lower legs of the breeches were fixed with buttons, and straps beneath the feet. Note that the lower part of the pocket is double-sewn for extra strength.

Binoculars. *The armed forces used 6x30 field binoculars, the lenses marked with artillery graticules for measuring range. The left and right lenses could be focused separately. The binoculars were carried in a leather case which could be worn either on the belt or slung on a shoulder strap. This early piece has a cheaper but still well made strengthened canvas case on a canvas webbing strap.*

The stampings on the binocular body show the serial number and the year of manufacture (here 1932), separated by the Army mark of the star and hammer-and-sickle. Below this is the prism sign used on optical equipment to identify the factory. This pentagonal prism with an arrow symbolising the route of the light is the trademark of Leningrad

Optical Mechanical Union (GOMZ, later LOMO). They also used a mark of the Kremlin tower with a star on the top. Another famous military optic supplier was the Krasnogorsk Mechanical Factory in the suburbs of Moscow (KMZ, later GOMZ); their stamped mark was an arrow on a trapezoid prism, or an arrow with wings. If there is no year stamp on optical equipment it is usually suggested by the first two digits of the serial number.

FIRE BRIGADE

Fire Brigade helmet, 1925. *Fire Brigade units were also under the command of the NKVD. Its Main Division was under the personal command of the Secretary of the NKVD (as were the Frontier Guards, State Security, Militia and labour camps) from 10 July 1934.*

This commander's helmet was in use from 1925. Before then helmets were not standardised, and many kinds were in use - the remains of old Imperial stocks, locally made pieces, and others of foreign origin. This is a well designed piece with front and rear peaks to give maximum protection. Both iron and brass examples of the badge are known. Its design incorporates several traditional features: a horizontal ladder, fixing chains, crossed axes, fire hose, surrounded by flames and all surmounted by the hammer-and-sickle. The legend is 'Always Ready'. The straps and the liner are fixed to the helmet at the sides below the flaming grenade motifs. Note the chin strap, incorporating large leather flaps on both sides to protect the ears; the nearside end has been broken and its owner has repaired it with an early wristwatch bracelet.

(Right) Fire Brigade badge, enlisted ranks, 1927. *This badge was worn on the collar patches; however, because no other badge was issued for the everyday and working hats of enlisted firemen, this piece was also used as a cap badge from 1927. The commanders' visored cap badge (introduced 1923) was similar, but with two axes and two crossed red enamelled flags at the top.*

THE GREAT PATRIOTIC WAR, 1941-45
NKVD

NKVD Commanders, Sochi, 1941. These security service officers (the central and right hand men are NKVD officers, the left hand man is the same Militia officer as illustrated on pages 9, 14 & 15) are relaxing at the Armed Forces Sanatorium in the famous Black Sea summer health resort and spa near Yalta. The central officer is probably of high rank; he wears NKVD patches on both sleeves (see also page 17), but his collar patches lack rank insignia. To omit the display of rank badges, or even to wear civilian clothes, was a usual method for the privileged officers of the NKVD to confuse, frustrate or frighten civilians or members of the other armed forces - the implication being that their authority was such that their relative rank was irrelevant. They were 'outside the system'; they did not have to take orders from anyone, but could give orders - or 'advice' - to anyone. Note the cap bands and collar patches: Militia (here) light blue, and NKVD brick red.

(Right) NKVD State Security cap. The band and the piping to the dark blue top are raspberry red; and note the 'square' shape of the visor, typical of the period. By now the top was generally worn stiffened flat.

(Bottom right) NKVD Frontier Guards cap. The top is green piped with raspberry red; the band appears black but is actually very dark blue. All ranks had black chin straps. The cap badge worn by all services except the Militia was the regular Army-type red-enamelled brass star with hammer-and-sickle.

(Below) NKVD collar patches. These are of the pattern worn on the winter coat by enlisted ranks. Note the raspberry red piping on the upper edges; the ground of NKVD brick red; and the rear strengthened with canvas. The branch symbol is for NKVD infantry - in practice, 'general service'. For higher ranks the appropriate geometrically-shaped red-enamelled emblems were added under the branch symbol in a horizontal row.

SERGEANT, FIELD DRESS, AUTUMN 1941

(Above) The gymnastiorka. *This shows the details of the external pockets, the black iron field buttons, and the brick red collar patches with raspberry red piping and the single triangular symbol of this rank. Notice the cut of the gymnastiorka; the lower part fell far below the waist and was almost as wide as a skirt - much wider than the shoulders.*

(Below) The budionovka. *This is an enlisted ranks' piece; there is no edging to the brick red cloth star, and the buttons are of black-painted iron. The top is low compared to earlier pieces; this reflects both economies in manufacture, and practicality - the low-pointed pattern was more stable on the head. The visor has also become smaller since the 1920s.*

This sergeant displays the brick red NKVD distinguishing colour on his collar patches and budionovka. Another less obvious NKVD feature is that his breast pockets are of patch type, i.e. externally fixed; those of the Red Army-style gymnastiorka were usually internal, with only the buttoned flap visible. This rule of 'external pockets for internal state security uniforms' was often broken in practice due to shortages. For the same reason, although he is a career sergeant he has an enlisted ranks' single-prong belt. His map case is slung well below his waist belt, as was usual in these early years. His weapon is the M1930 TT (Tula-Tokarev) 7.62mm semi-automatic pistol. This image is probably typical of the appearance of the NKVD personnel who murdered thousands of captured Polish officers in Katyn forest in 1939 or 1940.

— 23 —

OFFICER, 1942

(Left) This officer has the regular NKVD visored hat and a long, double-breasted leather coat. The latter was typically used by State Security officers and Air Force pilots in this period. As was usual during the 1930s and the Patriotic War, he wears no rank insignia when at the front or 'working' with civilian suspects and enemies of the Soviet state. He wears the general issue officers' M1935 belt set with cut-out star buckle. The book he carries is the 'Life of Stalin'.

CAPTAIN, 1943

(Right) His cap is conventional; but his tunic conforms with the radical new uniform regulations of early 1943, which restored the standing collar and shoulderboards of rank which had been discarded at the time of the Revolution. The Red Army, Red Air Force and Red Fleet received the new orders as Prikaz No.25 dated 15 January 1943; the NKVD, as their separate Prikaz No.126 of 18 February, signed by Lavrenti Beria, the Chief Commissar of State Security. The NKVD is identified by the dark blue piping on the shoulderboards now displayed on his kitel tunic, and also on his standing collar and cuffs; his exact rank, by the single central stripe and four stars on the shoulderboards. Since he is on duty he uses a pair of khaki breeches instead of the everyday blue of the NKVD.

(Left) Junior Sergeant, Internal Forces, spring 1943. This picture shows the very moment when the shoulderboards were reintroduced and first issued to NKVD personnel and front-line Red Army units. These shoulderboards have been fitted to an old fall-collar gymnastiorka *probably left in stock from the 1920s, to judge by the long collar points and the inconveniently large pockets (see page 16).*

(Right) Sergeant, Internal Forces, summer 1943. This photograph was taken in a trench - an unusual place for NKVD personnel. As a member of an elite unit he is well equipped, with a PPSh41 7.62mm sub-machine gun, stick grenades, and binoculars (in the Red Army optical equipment was normally given only to officers). His M1940 helmet has a painted red star. A variety of stars had been seen on helmets since the Revolution. In the early years added metal stars were preferred (on the French-made Adrian and on some 'Finnish' M1916 helmets); these followed the pre-Revolutionary method for fixing the Imperial eagle badge. Later the star was painted solid, as here, or in outline only (see Book 1, the M1936 helmet on page 24). No doubt the fully painted red star was impressive, but it was also danger-ously visible as an aiming mark; in time its display was limited to parade occasions. Note the painted numbers and letters on his shoulder-boards. Here field quality khaki breeches are worn instead of blue sharovary.

(Above) Lieutenant-Colonel, NKVD, c.1944. Even in black and white pictures it is easy to see the dark blue top of the hat, in contrast with the red band and piping. He wears the wartime officers' M1943 spring/autumn topcoat. This was made from a poor quality lightweight material, with no cuff piping or sleeve patches; it had two rows of three buttons. Note that his rank stars are not fixed to the stripes on the shoulderboard but directly to the base material on the outer parts of the boards.

(Right) Master Sergeant and Sergeant-Major, NKVD, 1945. While the master sergeant wears the enlisted ranks' belt and khaki breeches, the sergeant-major has the officers' two-prong field belt and blue sharovary with red officers' piping. The sleeve chevrons, of a type used between 1943 and 1947, indicate that he already has two years' service in the NKVD. Note the external patch pockets on the gymnastiorka.

SENIOR SERGEANT, SUMMER 1944

Behind the front lines, the white gymnastiorka, blue sharovary and coloured visored cap give him maximum visibility among the khaki-clad mass of Red Army troops. Note his excellent quality boots and the loose cut of his breeches. As a career sergeant he has similar equipment to his officers: an officer's map case, belt and sidearm. The old Nagant revolver was fixed around the neck with a special lanyard, a traditional feature for Internal Forces units and Militia personnel going back to the time of Imperial regulations. (The photograph was taken by my friend Gyula Jászberény only a few days before his death.)

(Below) The new M943 shoulderboard for enlisted ranks. Senior Sergeant, 8th NKVD (Infantry) Regiment. Note that in contrast to Red Army practice NKVD troops most often wore any cyphers close to the neck end and any rank stripes close to the shoulder end. All applied insignia were silver-coloured, and the base of officers' parade shoulderboards was also silver. The piping was dark blue (here practically black) for NKVD troops.

MILITIAMAN, 1944

Militia units - in limited numbers - were also involved in front line operations. This policeman wears field uniform, but because of the lack of field quality (i.e. khaki) Militia shoulderboards he has attached a pair of everyday dark blue boards to the special Internal Forces field gymnastiorka with external pockets; in practice such units often used regular Red Army clothing. Note the extra wide cut of the field quality khaki breeches which here replace his everyday dark blue ones. As a career Militiaman rather than a temporary conscript he has the officers' belt and binoculars. His weapon is the 7.62mm DP (Degtyarev) squad light machine gun, carried on a canvas sling.

V.A.Degtyarev received the second award of the Hero of Socialist Labour Order in 1940 for his invention of this weapon. The first award of the order - unsurprisingly - was to Stalin, a few days earlier in 1939, for his 60th birthday. This decoration, the civilian version of the military Hero of the USSR award, has an added hammer-and-sickle on the gold star.

(Above) *The M1943 shoulderboard for a Militia enlisted man, of everyday quality in Militia dark blue with light blue piping and the silver cypher of a '10th' unit of some kind.*

MILITIA CAPTAIN 'ON DUTY', SPRING 1944

This officer wears the single-breasted everyday dark blue mundir *tunic, piped red at collar and cuffs, complete with* Patrul *(patrol) brassard, and matching red-piped breeches. Before 1947 all Militia officers' shoulderboards were silver-coloured; note the red piping and contrasting gold rank stars.*

From 1936 onwards the cap badge for commanders was a round coat of arms, which replaced the former insginia of a blue star with a small coat of arms in the middle. Officially a red star with the coat of arms was introduced in 1939, but the larger badge illustrated here countinued in use until 1947, when the oval officers' badge was standardised. Note that the shoulder brace of the partupey *('Sam Browne') belt kit was not always worn for city service. He displays a Red Star Order for injury, and a medal for the 20th Anniversary of the Armed Forces in 1938.*

(Below) Militia commanders' metal sleeve badge, 1936. While it was very rare to see sleeve insignia in the Red Army at this time, NKVD officers had various arm badges. As we have seen, State Security officers wore on both sleeves a shield-and-sword patch (see pages 17 & 21); and Militia commanders displayed this metal badge of the coat of arms of the USSR on the left upper sleeve (see page 15) - the only metal arm badge in Soviet military history. It was a slightly larger version of the cap badge for officers introduced under the same order of 15 June 1936 (see main photograph on this page). Militia political commissars wore instead an embroidered turquoise blue star with gold piping and the hammer-and-sickle emblem.

MAJOR, NKVD MEDICAL SERVICE, SPRING 1945

This female medical officer is checking the health status of the returning sailors, soldiers and prisoners of war at the strategic Baltic Fleet port of Kronstadt near Leningrad. This is a hot weather parade uniform for female officers of the NKVD: a single-breasted, stand-collar kitel *tunic 'for female command personnel of organs of NKVD of the USSR', with dark blue skirt and beret and the officers' belt. The narrow shoulderboards were characteristic of administrative and medical officers. Berets were introduced to the Soviet armed forces in August 1941 exclusively for female personnel; the top was made from one piece, the sides from four quarters. Female berets were especially worn by non-combatant command personnel with everyday or parade uniforms. Her brassard identifies her as an 'officer on duty at headquarters'. She has a Victory over Germany medal on her left, and on her right is a medical badge for 'Excellent Worker of Public Health Care of the USSR'. This silver badge with gold details was established in 1935; later variously sized exampes were issued in silver, bronze and aluminium (in 1938, and 1960).*

(Below) Young Excellent Defender of Public Health Care of the USSR. *This health care badge was established in 1938, and appeared in various other versions in the following decades.*

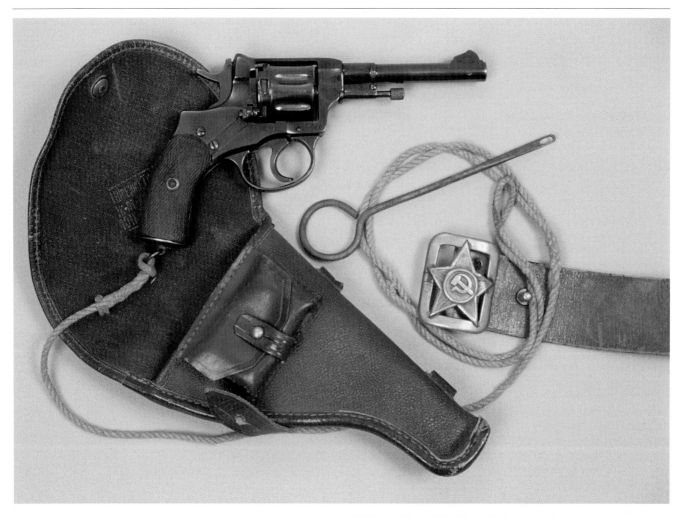

(Above) The Nagant M1895 revolver. This old-fashioned weapon remained basically unchanged after World War I. Originally designed by the Belgian engineer L.Nagant and introduced in the Russian Empire in 1895, it was used in large quantities until the end of World War II, especially by State Security, Militia and naval officers, and armed security guards at strategic factories and power stations. It was of 7.62mm calibre, had triple-groove rifling, weighed 0.75kg (1.65lbs), and - unusually - the cylinder held seven rounds instead of the more common six. The sights were modified in 1930. Later, shortened versions and others in 5.6mm calibre were also made, mostly for training and sports shooting. With a maximum useful range of 100 metres it was not as accurate as, and far less effective than, the TT semi-automatic, but it was still in service in the early 1950s.

(Right) Internal Forces Service Regulations, 1945-46. This book of regulations was published in Moscow. Internal Forces documents such as regulations, personal records, certificates and photographs are rarer than Ministry of Defence printed materials due to tighter security, more limited print runs, and the usual practice of destroying them after changes made them obsolete. Note the new ministry title on this example: the short-lived Ministry of the Armed Forces.

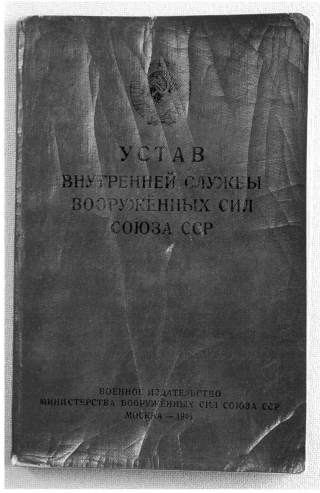

(Right) The movie is over - 1945. NKVD officers in walking-out uniforms at an open air cinema. Note that they wear no belts, since they are 'out of formation'. Militia and Internal Forces troops had removable white summer covers for the visored cap, which could be worn from May Day until 1 September each year. Between 15 October and 15 March the ushanka *winter hat was in use; and in spring and autumn the visored cap without a white cover. In various climatic areas the regulations could be changed by order of the territory commander. Note that these officers display medal ribbons only, in place of the full medals - a practice followed in 1945-46, which required ribbons to be designed for the first time for orders previously worn as pin-on decorations.*

(Below) Master Sergeant, NKVD Internal Forces, in the liberated Ukraine, 1945. The gymnastiorka *has, irregularly, no collar buttons. The meaning of the cypher 'UVV' painted on his shoulderboards is 'Internal Forces (of the Soviet Republic of the) Ukraine'; almost invisible above this is the number of the 240th (Infantry) Battalion.*

In the territory of the liberated Ukraine, especially in the western regions, partisan warfare continued, but this time against the Soviet Union. Various groups were made up of Soviet deserters, former collaborators with the German occupation, Ukrainian nationalists and former partisans, and simply local people. The largest group was the UPA, the Ukrainian Uprising (or Rebel) Army.

The Soviet state security forces carried out large scale military operations against these groups in an extremely bloody fratricidal struggle which lasted until the mid-1950s. The 'partisans' had a mixture of wartime German or German auxiliary uniforms with Ukrainian nationalist insignia, and civil clothing; sometimes, unexpectedly, they were seen in regular Soviet uniforms - including brand new Soviet Air Force clothing, or most strangely of all, in NKVD, later MVD and MGB uniforms. After the end of World War II they managed to kill thousands of soldiers and officers in various, but especially state security units; but also state bureaucrats, party functionaries, collective farm managers, village council members, and anyone else co-operating with the Soviet power structure. They also inflicted major damage on agriculture, industry, transport and communications.

medals and badges of many other 'Socialist' states were entirely or partly made by the Moscow or Leningrad Mints, e.g. those of Mongolia, Cuba and Afghanistan.)

This ribbon set includes several wartime orders, e.g. in order of appearance from top left the Orders of Lenin, the Red Banner, the Patriotic War 1st and 2nd Classes, and two awards of the Red Star. Other wartime ribbons recognisable here include the Combat Service, Defender of Leningrad and Victory over Germany medals. (Some homework for readers: try to identify all of them…)

Finally, it should be said that the unbelievable quantity of medals and orders awarded in World War II was largely due to the unbelievable quality of performance, bravery and self-sacrifice of the Soviet armed forces, where manpower often had to make up for shortages of technology, fuel, ammunition or even weapons.

(Right) Ribbon set of a Great Patriotic War veteran. Because of the unbelievable variety of medals awarded, at the end of and immediately after World War II ribbons were worn alone on everyday and field uniforms - a change from traditional Russian practice. As well as new ribbons for Soviet orders, some foreign orders also received ribbon equivalents at this period; e.g. the Mongolian Polar Star Order, which was also awarded to some Soviet forces personnel for wartime service. (It is worth noting that the

SERGEANT-MAJOR, MILITIA, FAR EAST, 1945

This is the double-breasted parade version of the M1943 mundir tunic, worn with matching cap and breeches, all in blue piped with raspberry red. As a professional career NCO he wears the officer's version of the tunic, but without the collar and cuff patches with silver metallic lace bars, which were only for officers. The shoulderboards have the T-shaped rank stripes of sergeant-major in silver lace. This former front-line fighter has just returned from the short campaign against Japan in Manchuria. Note the Victory over Japan Medal - the last one of the row, which otherwise comprises the Order of Glory 3rd Class, the Bravery Medal, the silver Medal for Military Merit, and the brass Victory over Germany Medal. Note the sergeants' belt set with traditional shaska sabre; officially all parts of the leather set should be the same shade.

Invitation leaflet and tribune (dais) ticket for the Red Square Victory Over Germany Parade, 24 June 1945. *This famous event included the throwing down of captured German flags as a slighting of Nazi symbols. The march-past by all kinds of Soviet troops included many who had not* long returned from the bloody battle for Berlin a few weeks previously, as well as the début of a military cadet band recruited from war orphans. A firework display that night was followed by a choreographed 'dance' by the beams of hundreds of high powered anti-aircraft searchlights (replacing the originally planned aerial fly-past, cancelled due to lack of fuel). It is interesting to note that the USSR was not at war with Japan at this date, so a Japanese military and political delegation was invited to the parade along with the representatives of the Allies and many other neutral nations; war was declared on Japan only on 8 August, two days after the American atom bomb was dropped on Hiroshima. The leaflet was issued by Kuznetsov, the USSR Commissar for State Security, whose committee controlled and planned the parade.

NKVD Frontier Guards

CAPTAIN, 1945

Seen here (right hand figure) with a Red Army major wearing the same M1943 parade uniform, the Frontier Guards officer is distinguished by his green-topped cap, and green collar patches and piping on his mundir. The double-breasted cut identifies a combat unit; the Army major belongs to the Supply Corps, and his non-combatant service is indicated by his single-breasted tunic. Field grade officers - majors, lieutenant-colonels and colonels - had double metallic lace bars on the cuffs and collar patches; captains and lieutenants had only single bars. These parade uniforms could be worn with or without the leather belt. The breeches are blue - of differing shades - with piping in branch colours. In the rear view note the old-fashioned cut, with piped false pockets harking back to the Napoleonic period; and the position of the belt, supported by the upper buttons.

(Above) Enlisted ranks' **budionovka, 1941.** *While earlier types of* budionovka *were rather browner (see page 16), this piece is grey to harmonise with the colour and material of the winter coat of the period. From 1941 the* ushanka *type winter hat was the official issue, but the* budionovka *could still be seen in occasional use in the later war years.*

THE COLD WAR, 1945-91
MVD - Ministry of Internal Affairs

The Ministry of Internal Affairs (or 'of the Interior'), known by the abbreviation MVD, was the successor to the NKVD. On 15 March 1946 an order of the Supreme Soviet of the USSR abolished all the former People's Committees and replaced them - for the first time in Soviet history - with Ministries. The three armed services - their titles also being changed that year, from 'Red Army' to 'Soviet Army', etc. - came under the control of the Ministry of the Armed Forces. In 1950 this was divided into the Ministry of the Army and Ministry of the Navy, but in 1953 these were once more unified as the Ministry of Defence.

The former NKVD, responsible for internal security, thus became on 15 March 1946 the Ministry of Internal Affairs, which retained responsibility for internal security and law enforcement until the end of the USSR. For a short period between 1962 and 1968, after several structural changes, it was named the Ministry for the Protection of Public Order (MOOP). The MVD had the usual functions, its departments, sections, bureaus and offices being tasked with preserving public order and guarding the property of the state, protecting the interests and rights of Soviet citizens and organisations. The MVD's mission embraced the struggle against all kinds of anti-social activity, whether criminal or terrorist, but also the response to such natural disasters as fire, earthquake and flood. Its personnel served in many different uniformed branches, including Militia, Transport Militia, anti-terrorist units (OMON), Internal Forces (VV), special operations units (Spetznaz), fire brigades and civil defence teams.

Militia

(Top right) Traffic Militia Officers, 1947. Traffic and Water Militia uniform differed from other police branches after the 1943 uniform reforms. The main difference was their red-topped visored caps with black bands, which could be held in the hand to signal to cars or even trains. In summer the red top was covered by a removable, washable white cover. Between 1943 and 1947 they had double-breasted uniforms, simplified from the latter year with single-breasted tunics. While other police units had blue uniforms before c.1970, the transport units nearly always wore black clothing, though blue was sometimes seen due to shortages. Railway police wore the emblem of a crossed hammer and monkey-wrench; waterways patrols officially wore an anchor as their shoulderboard emblem under the 1943 regulations, but this was not always seen in practice.

This junior lieutenant (right) wears a brassard identifying him as 'officer on duty'. Shaska swords were often worn in the absence of truncheons. He has regulation spurs on his excellent boots. The lowest officer rank of one-star junior lieutenant was still in use in the armed forces until the end of the USSR, but in the post-war years practically all cadets were graduated by the academies as at least two-star lieutenants.

(Middle right) Traffic Militia General's winter hat, 1947. (Militia generals were officially termed 'commissars'.) The oval general officers' cockade badge was introduced in this year. The black colour was used for papaha hats until 1958, when it was replaced by grey, similar to Army generals' winter headgear. Colonels had the same hat but with a dark blue top with a red cross instead of the red and gold which distinguished generals.

(Bottom right) Enlisted ranks' belt buckle, 1947. The Militia introduced the brass buckle plate for the leather service belt slightly earlier than the Soviet Army; in the Army it was general issue only from 1951, being seen worn only by cadets before that date. While on Army buckles, buttons, sleeve patches and cap badges the star with hammer-and-sickle was the dominant motif, the Militia favoured the coat of arms of the USSR as shown here, which appeared on various parts of the uniform in different periods (e.g. as a collar emblem, and sometimes on buttons and cap badges). Only limited numbers of this rare belt buckle survived the period, since from 1951 the Militia in practice made much use of the more available Army style, especially the transport police branches (see photograph page 38); and also because after the mid-1960s most enlisted personnel preferred the more prestigious officers' 'Sam Browne' belt with a two-prong frame buckle. This buckle with the coat of arms was mentioned for the last time in the 1965 regulations.

Note that early and wartime-made Soviet buckles were often fixed to the right hand end of the leather, and post-war buckles to the left hand end. This is an aid to identification, of e.g. wartime Red Fleet buckles from later Soviet naval pieces.

(Left) Militia NCOs, early 1950s. Their uniforms are black or dark blue (both were in use during this period.) While the sergeant-major on duty (right) has the leather officers' belt set, two others (second left, second right) have the new coat-of-arms buckles. Note the less than smart sergeant-major (left), wearing an Army-style belt upside down; he is also wearing a warm but old and worn-out M1943 tunic without collar patches as winter clothing. The junior sergeant (second left) also shows some irregularity of dress, with his officers' coat with red piping around the collar and front edge. Another irregular feature is the naval TT pistol holster worn on the everyday belt by the sergeant (second right).

(Left) Traffic Militia personnel, 1959. Note the sleeve patch of the junior sergeant (right). When introduced in 1943 the traffic sleeve patch bore the three letters 'RUD' ('Traffic Control Service'); but for a short period from 1957 it was simplified to one letter, a gold metal or yellow-painted 'T' (Transport) on a dark blue cloth diamond piped in red. As seen here, this was used only by enlisted ranks; officers wore no arm patch. While the Soviet Army had already adopted collar patch emblems on their coats since 1955, the police still used buttons only; in 1965 these were finally replaced by collar emblems.

(Right) Militia NCOs, c.1945. *Despite their rank these off-duty police sergeants and sergeant-majors wear the red-piped double-breasted officers' M1943 parade tunic, as shown on page 34.*

(Below) Militia personnel, 1950s. *Both single- and double-breasted tunics are visible in this photo of officers and NCOs at a meeting dominated by a noticeboard headed 'Historic Decisions of the 20th Party Congress' - this was the 1956 Congress at which Stalin's crimes and cult of personality were denounced for the first time.*

MILITIA CAPTAIN, 1958

The darker blue uniform differs in colour from those of the World War II period, and the visored cap is worn with the M1947 oval badge. Medals are not worn, only ribbons (if any). This is the last time that the mundir with a closed standing collar and removable shoulderboards was ordered for use. A new generation of open-collared tunics with fixed (sewn on) shoulderboards was already being introduced in this year, initially for generals, and became common for all ranks after 1965. He carries a gramophone record with the National Anthems of the USSR and the Soviet Republics.

(Opposite top) Officers, 1958. While the Army introduced in 1955 the open-collared parade tunic, MVD personnel still had the old standing-collar version with red cuff piping until 1958. In this group only the woman at front centre has received the new pattern issued in this year. The regulations mentioned a single-breasted type for female commanders, but this is clearly a double-breasted tunic with piping around the collar and on the cuffs. Her shoulderboards bear the three stars of senior lieutenant's rank. Those of the other officers are visibly of the 'hexagonal' removable pattern (i.e. the old shape with the inner end clipped to three short, straight edges); these were soon to be replaced with sewn-down boards cut to a single angled edge at the inner end, obscured on many garments by the fall collar. Note that there is only one wartime hero in this group, with two rows of medal ribbons.

(Below) Visored cap, M1947. The oval cap badge introduced in 1947 in officers' and enlisted ranks' versions - note the blue central cartouche bearing the hammer-and-sickle. The cap crown is dark blue; and note the small size of the visor.

(Left) Militia General, Commissar 3rd Class, 1965. The new open-collar Militia uniforms with fixed shoulderboards introduced in 1958 appeared first in the form of parade dress. This senior officer wears a mixture of everyday and parade uniform pieces of the period, especially for a visit to the photographer's studio. The tunic and visored cap are for everyday use; they were similar to the parade items in their dark blue colour, but the true parade tunic had more decoration on the collar, with both silver and red piping. Later, the general officers' everyday and especially parade caps had more ornamentation around the cockade (see colour photograph, page 48).

The everyday uniform was worn with a blue shirt and a leather belt, but here they have been replaced with a parade belt and white shirt. He also sports a full display of medals instead of the ribbons only. The cap badge, the parade belt, the shoulderboards and the collar ornaments for Militia generals are silver-coloured. The cut of the collar shown here differs from the later version (see colour photograph on page 48). Note the old-style 1940 vintage silver NKVD badge pinned to his right lapel. Militia generals had special titles (see table below), Officers below general, and enlisted ranks, used Army-style ranks, though starting with 'Policeman' - Militioner. The Militia and Customs Service had entirely career personnel; all other services included short-service conscripts of military age.

Stars	Militia	Army, VV, PV, KGB
One	Commissar 3rd Class	Major-General
Two	Commissar 2nd Class	Lieutenant-General
Three	Commissar 1st Class	Colonel-General

(Left) Excellent MVD Militiaman badge, M1948. This is a later bronze version of the badge first issued in 1946 with the change of title; the abbreviation shown at the bottom changed from 'NKVD' to 'MVD', as here; and in a later version, from 1962, to 'MOOP'. The first numbered award certificates of the NKVD version from October 1940, issued and signed by the head of the NKVD, were inscribed 'For Effective Work Fulfilling the Special Mission of Law Enforcement'.

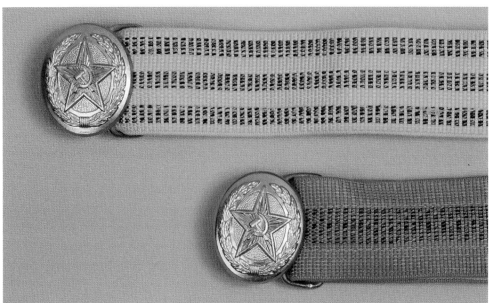

(Left) Parade belts and buckles. From the 1955 uniform reforms the male parade uniforms of all the armed forces were worn with a gold-embroidered fabric parade belt. While the regular officers' parade belt was light-coloured with three dark stripes for all services (e.g. Internal Forces, Soviet Army, Air Force, Fire Brigade), the sole exception was the Militia, which from 1975 used this darker-coloured belt with one central dark stripe - see the lower example. The brass buckles were the same.

(Above left and right) Militia motorcycle outriders, c.1960. Photographed during a 7 November winter parade, they wear various protective clothing - many seem to have old-style Air Force warm overalls. They also have old-style Air Force headgear (one on the right of the posing group has a new helmet with an integral intercom system), and new goggles with dark green plastic sun guards over the top of the lenses. The parading convoy carries the flags of the Warsaw Pact countries. The legend on the ribbon of the leader is 'Champion of the USSR'.

(Below) Militia motorcyclist parade helmet badges. Large badges like that at top left were displayed from the mid-1970s on the white parade helmets of the police motorcyclists who escorted the cars of visiting delegations, or provided mobile security for parades on occasions such as May Day or the Anniversary of the October Revolution. At lower right is the Afghan police version, which is also believed to have been manufactured in Moscow or in Byelorussia by armed forces' badge companies in the early 1980s. The Soviet soldier's pilotka star and the standard Afghan soldier's cap badge are included at top right and lower left for scale comparison. After the mid-1950s most of the regular Soviet cap badges were made from lighter and cheaper aluminium instead of brass.

Militia training, mid-1960s.
Police personnel practising unarmed combat - in what appears to be a fairly relaxed mood - and on the pistol range. The uniforms may seem to contradict the activities, but until the late 1980s the Militia had no 'combat' clothing.

MILITIA VISORED CAPS:

(Right) Officers', everyday, M1965. The badge is not as narrow as the M1947. Note that this example still does not have a stiffened flat top.

(Right) Enlisted ranks', everyday, M1969. The colour has now become grey, like the shoulderboards and the uniform itself. The cap still has a black chin strap, and no ornamentation around the cockade. The crown is now stiffened.

(Right) Officers', summer, M1977. The white top for this class of cap was introduced for summer use in 1970. (Various other NKVD caps with white tops were already in use as early as the 1920s.). The badge with ornamental leaves flanking the cockade appeared from 1977. The crown is stiffened, and raised at the front.

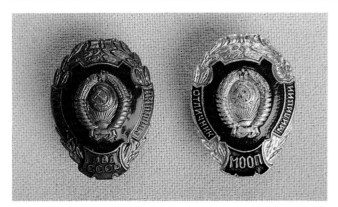

(Above left) **Excellent MVD and MOOP Militiaman badges, 1953 and 1962.** *The brass badge was made with the legend 'MVD' at the bottom, briefly replaced from 1962 with 'MOOP'. Another version also from 1962 was marked 'Excellent Internal Forces Service, MOOP' and awarded to VV troops.*

(Above centre) **Excellent MVD Militiaman, 1970.** *This aluminium badge replaced the earlier ones in 1970, when the re-organisation of the MOOP led to the restoration of the 'MVD' legend.*

(Above right) **Excellent MVD Propagandist, early 1980s.** *This was given for outstanding work in the fields of propaganda, education and politico-ideological activities. Although it was instituted by a central MVD prikaz (order), no exact date for its introduction has been found.*

(Above) **Propaganda.** *This picture is a reminder of the ubiquitous symbols of state propaganda in the daily life of the Soviet Union in the 'Brezhnev era' of the 1970s. Workplaces, classrooms, hospitals, Army bases and Militia stations were just some of the venues lavishly decorated with pictures and slogans promoting the advantages and superiority of 'Socialist' life. Streets and walls were decorated with reliefs, plaques and statues, and in parks and boulevards actual tanks, aircraft, rockets, cannons, even armoured trains were displayed as monuments. Radio, newspapers, public address systems, films, and later TV programmes constantly assured the population that theirs was the best possible way of life.*

It is interesting to consider the 'cycles' of these symbols. At the time of the Revolution and during World War II such exhortations had real meaning; but later they often lost their impact and seemed mere empty

(Above) **Symbolism in everyday life.** *Small souvenirs were popular in every family, like the Kremlin in stone, plastic, glass or silver, or this toy Maxim machine gun. State power was largely based on the trust, co-operation, support*

and belief of the citizens; practically the entire society was voluntarily involved in the system and took advantage from it. Celebrated poets such as Mayakovski wrote in heroic terms about the Soviet police, and the Soviet passport, and his pride in being a Soviet citizen when visiting England in the 1920s. Books, films, even children's tales were all designed to help the people distinguish good from bad and to live their lives by a new kind of rules: Socialist co-existence. A certain wariness is in order when we read today, after the fall of Communism, how many people claim to have actively resisted the system, and to have suffered as a consequence - the Gulag was real enough, of course, but a number of self-proclaimed 'sufferers' enjoyed positions of high privilege in the Soviet era.

noise. It is bizarre to see gigantic slogans which it has proved physically impossible to remove from factory walls even ten years after the fall of the system: 'Glory to Work, Friendship between Peoples and Nations, Peace'. They had no impact in the 1980s because they were taken for granted. Now, when former industrial regions are suffering gross unemployment, minorities are not always regarded with tolerance, and millions of Russians are living in the newly 'foreign' post-Soviet states, these slogans have more meaning than ever.

The photograph shows a police station interior in the 1970s. On the walls are portraits of Leonid Ilyich Brezhnev, Secretary of the Communist Party, and of members of the Politbureau and the Central Committee. There is a poster on the life of Lenin, and a leaflet: 'Moral Code for Communists'. In the corner is the flag of the Militia unit with the usual text: 'Workers of the World Unite!'

Pictures from the secret personal dossiers of Militia personnel, mid-1980s:

(Left) Sergeant, parade uniform. It is worn with a white shirt and gold-edged collar patches. Note his sleeve patch.

(Right) Sergeant-Major, parade uniform. Note that he wears an everyday tunic without gold collar patch edging. His medals are displayed without any systematic order (although there were strict regulations about the order of precedence, and the distance they were to be worn from the collar, first button, etc, in millimetres). The badges on his right breast are '25th Anniversary of the Victory over Nazi Germany' and 'Excellent MVD Militiaman' (see opposite), both from 1970. He has the 20 Year Service Medal; such long service almost always brought the automatic award of every jubilee medal issued during the individual's years of service; by contrast, some higher ranking officers with relatively short service time had no medals.

(Left) Cadet from a Central Asian Republic. Note the wide edge stripes and the 'K' on his shoulderboards. Because he is under 25 years old he is still a member of the Communist Party Youth Organisation (Komsomol) and wears its badge on his left breast.

(Right) Lieutenant. Note his unusual MVD academy and secondary school badges. In the late 1980s some graduation badges were not of the usual diamond shape, and changed in design from year to year to mark special events such as the 30th graduating class of the institute, etc. Irregularities here are the everyday *kitel* worn with a parade white shirt, and the short shoulderboards.

(Left) Criminal Investigator Lieutenant. His collar patches bear the legal branch emblem. He also has a State Security Academy badge, with the portrait of Felix Dzerzhinsky and a sword. The buttons on the shoulderboards are now purely decorative. Militia winter coats also had decorative buttons on the cuffs.

(Right) Female Criminal Investigator Senior Lieutenant. Note the different cut of the collar and position of the patches - this arrangement was originally for enlisted ranks. She too has the investigation officers' collar emblem, and the Excellent MVD Militioner *badge from 1970.*

(Left) *The correct collar shape and placement of patches for female Militia officers — compare with the portrait above.*

MILITIA GENERAL, 1981

Irregularly, this Commissar 3rd Class wears a white parade shirt with everyday double-breasted uniform, as sometimes seen. On the parade tunic the shoulderboards would be of gold lace, and he would display a full set of medals instead of these ribbons. From 1969 the Militia uniform changed colour from blue to grey, with red pipings and generals' stripes on the straight trousers. He wears international medals from Bulgaria, Romania, and other Socialist countries in the lower two rows; he has presumably served as a liaison officer with the security forces of these states. He has also been injured in action, since he wears the ribbon of the Red Star Order. Before this he wears the blue ribbons of two awards of the Red Banner of Labour; such multiple awards were rare by this date. In order to combat the 'cult of personality' in the post-Stalin era most awards were given to individuals only once. Only extreme heroism justified a second award of the same order, e.g. the space missions of the Cosmonauts. Note the General Staff Academy badge on his right breast, with gold edging, instead of the white-edged diamond of the Officers' Academy badge .

(Below) Militia Generals' caps, early 1980s. The embroidered ornamentation around the cockade was introduced for generals in 1969. The darker grey cap was worn with the tunic; the lighter grey, in summer with the light grey shirtsleeve order (with long sleeves from 1975, with short sleeves from 1984).

FEMALE MAJOR, TRAFFIC MILITIA, TASHKENT, 1986

In tropical regions such as the Soviet Asian Republics everyday working uniform comprised lighter, short-sleeved versions of summer uniforms, especially from the 1970s. This traffic police major has a light blue one-piece dress with an integral belt of the same material, introduced in 1975. The summer pilotka *head-gear, in grey with red piping, was ordered for wear by female personnel from 1977. The shoulderboards are removable. The brass buttons were replaced with plastic from 1987. No holster or side case is worn with this uniform. Note the breast badge; the Soviet driving licence in her hand; the truncheon, which was always black-and-white; and the white Lada car used by Militia.*

(Below) Traffic control person-nel and police breast badges. *This 90x70mm red badge (left) was introduced for traffic control inspectors and policemen on duty in 1985. The upper legend flanking the coat of arms of the USSR on both badges is the abbreviation for 'Ministry of Internal Affairs', 'USSR'. The large characters on the left badge, 'GAI', stand for 'State Traffic Control'; below them are an area code and the officer's personal number, for identification when on duty out on the road. The police badge on the right lacks these per-sonalised details; the wearers served in a Militia building, and different individuals wore it during their shifts on duty.*

(Far left) Enlisted ranks' specialist badge, M1955. *This series of badges with red shields was introduced a year later than the parallel Ministry of Defence specialist series in blue.*

(Left) Officers' Specialist wings, M1978. *Note that the 'M' (Master) grade usually included in Army specialist badge series did not exist in Militia badge sets.*

(Below) Militia medals: (left) 50th Anniversary of the Militia, *awarded from 1967, usu-* ally for 25 years' service, or 'for officers and servicemen with impeccable service reputation', or 'for active helpers of the Militia'. It was awarded annually on 10 November, which was Soviet Militia Day.

(Right) 'For Distinguished Service in the Maintenance of Public Order', *awarded from 1950 to Militia and Internal Forces personnel and voluntary patrol members (see Druzhinniks, page 55). It could also be awarded to citizens for 'liquidation of criminal groups, arrest of criminals, crime prevention, organising operations, and struggle against crime, hooliganism, hard drinking and theft'. This rare medal, presented only by the highest authorities, was made of silver before 1960, and was later silver-plated.*

(Bottom left) Militia shoulderboards. *After 1969 the shoulderboards for all ranks had rounded inner ends, differing from those of all other services. The Militia retained buttons on all shoulderboards even when they were sewn to the uniform. The grey colour (here for senior lieutenant) replaced the former dark blue base colour on various types of shoulderboards gradually between 1965 and 1969. The gold base for parade uniforms came into use only in 1975. The Soviet coat of arms emblem was normally worn on the red collar patches. The only exception was the 'hexagonal'-cut shoulderboards worn with shirt-sleeve order. Since no collar patches were worn on the shirt, the Militia emblem was added next to the button on the shoulderboards.*

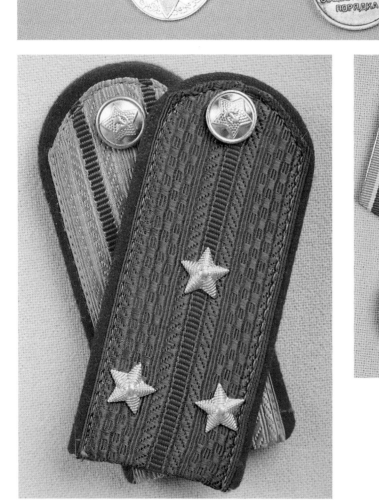

(Left) Medal 'For Strengthening of Combat Alliance', 1979. *Awarded to citizens of the USSR and other 'friendly states' who contributed to military, police and state security co-operation between the Socialist countries. As illustrated by the Militia general on page 48, every Communist country awarded similar medals for co-operation by 'brother country' officers. In the USSR this rarely awarded medal was given mostly to Soviet officers serving in Warsaw Pact states or as advisers in the Third World. It was also awarded to KGB and MVD personnel on foreign service or foreign training and exchange programmes.*

FEMALE CAPTAIN, MILITIA PARADE DRESS, 1987

The wool hat was introduced from 1984, with a slightly smaller badge for everyday use (see detail below) and this larger badge for parade dress. The new female parade uniform was introduced in 1987; it incorporated white shirt and gloves, black tie, gold-based shoulderboards, and all appropriate decorations and badges (here the specialist officer's wings, badge 'For Excellent MVD Service', academy graduation badge and 50th Anniversary of the Militia medal). A belt was not used with female parade dress. Note that for everyday uniforms female personnel had brown, for parades black tufli shoes. Uniform regulations for female personnel never omit to mention in the last chapter that 'it is strictly forbidden to wear shoes of unauthorised design or colour'.

(Below) M1984 female hat. Confusingly called a kepi, this hat was used in temperate weather with either parade (main picture) or everyday (here) badges.

(Above) Graduation badges.
(Top row) MVD academies and higher courses. The second, with the red banner and Lenin's portrait, is for higher political education; the small boat at the top of the badge is the symbol of Leningrad. The next, in the middle, is for MVD communication courses. Note that all MVD academy badges featured the sword and shield and coat of arms motifs.
(Second row) Schools of Marxism and Leninism; these were the highest instituions for political studies.

(Right) Middle grade badges.
This shape of badge was specifically for specialised secondary school students. These examples are for technical, MVD, art, literature and agricultural studies.

OMON - Militia Special Forces

After a number of internal crisis situations, ethnic conflicts and a rise in criminal activity, in the mid-1980s it became important to set up a new kind of Militia units, and equally to design a new generation of Internal Forces and MVD troops' field uniforms. The new organisation was named OMON (*Otdiela Militsii Osobovo Nazacheniya*, or Special Purpose Police Troops). Like the so-called *afghanka* uniforms produced for Army personnel and paratroopers fighting in Afghanistan (see *Book 1*), their new clothing was designed for functional utility. Before this new generation of clothing, as a sign of respect for the people of the 'First Socialist State', the Militia had never been seen on the streets of Moscow or Leningrad in field dress, but only in elegant walking-out style uniforms.

SENIOR SERGEANT, OMON, 1991

This type of new uniform was introduced by an MVD order in 1987; the example illustrated is a modified M1989 pattern. The combat cap, more practical in that it was harder to knock off during violent activity, was also a novelty, breaking the long traditional dominance of the visored cap. Note the smaller MVD badge, used both on combat caps and on female police headgear. The right to wear the blue and white striped undershirt had always been a privilege of sailors and elite units such as paratroopers and naval infantry, and its use by OMON troops underlined their special status. The OMON sleeve patch is similar to earlier ones worn on winter coats and police parade or walking-out uniforms, but slightly larger and bearing the legend 'MILITIA'. Note the unusual metal rank stripes replacing

the usual ribbon stripes on his very short shoulderboards. Metal stripes were first used from 1972, but initially only on enlisted ranks' everyday uniform shoulderboards. He displays a blood group patch over his right pocket; these have also been more widely seen on later Russian uniforms since 1991. This NCO has a special large holster for the Makarov pistol; the extra pocket on its face holds a silencer. The special pockets on the trousers, for 30-round AK74 magazines, remind us that OMON were trained to use heavier weapons than the militiaman's traditional pistol and truncheon. Note his cheap, shortened boots.

The light grey paint on metal and wooden items (here, the door) was typical for Ministry of Defence and Ministry of Internal Affairs bases and prisons.

(Above) Militia sleeve patches. Arm patches similar to those of the Soviet Army were worn only by enlisted ranks - officers never used them. There were no speciality patches, all bearing the same shield, sword, hammer-and-sickle motifs as the early embroidered NKVD patches of the 1930s. The left example here is for everyday uniform, the middle one for the coat and for parade and walking-out uniforms; both were introduced in 1977. The right hand patch is for OMON special units from 1988; the legend reads 'MILITIA', though one cannot help thinking that anyone close enough to read it was already in trouble.

(Right) Makarov semi-automatic pistol. Immediately following the Patriotic War, eight different new types of pistol were sent for testing to choose a replacement for the famous Tokarev TT, which had been on general issue since 1930 (with major modifications in 1933). The winner of the competition was the new weapon of Nikolai Fedorovich Makarov; it was lighter, smaller and safer under service conditions than the TT, it was effective at 50 metres' range, and its 9.2mm calibre was also a novelty. The PM.9.160/93.730.8.1. (to give it its full official name - probably the longest name ever for a small pistol!) was of a size and shape which made it more comfortable and easy to handle. This was one of the first Soviet handguns which was designed with an eye to its aesthetic and ergonomic qualities. After extensive trials it was finally accepted in late 1951. The magazine took eight rounds of the 9.2mm x 18mm ammunition (wrongly described in some sources as 9mm). Initially the cartridges had brass cases but later ammunition was produced from cheaper lacquered steel.

(Centre right) Early Makarov holster, 1953. This example was made from left-over artificial leather material as used for TT holsters and map cases in the late war years due to the shortage of natural leather; the added pocket carries a spare magazine. This piece demonstrates why it is rare to find stamped markings on World War II holsters, magazine pouches or map cases. The quality controller's stamp was often put on an added textile label (here dated 1953), which was immediately torn off by most users to prevent it snagging the pistol when it was drawn.

(Bottom right) Makarov holsters. The excellent quality larger example on the left is a later version for a pistol with silencer as used by OMON special forces. The right hand holster has the cleaning rod fixed with a key ring so as not to lose it during violent movement. The writing on the inside is the name of its former owner, Comrade Bessmertny. In English this Russian family name means 'Comrade Immortal' - a good name for a policeman! A white version of the holster was also in use for parades, and by traffic police and Army military police.

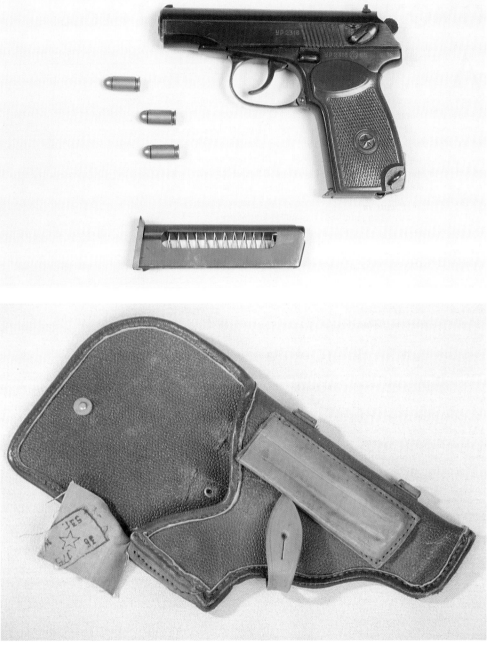

Militia Auxiliary Units

(Top right) **Voluntary Militia insignia.** The name for a voluntary helper of the Militia was Druzhinnik - *originally a term for the armed guards of medieval Tsars, and later used for the armed irregulars of the Revolution.* After the Revolution the members of volunteer civilian units kept the same historical name. Their function was to support professional units in dangerous situations; besides the Militia, specially trained volunteer units of the fire brigade, dog units and first aid groups were also formed to support the local authorities. The voluntary police units date back to 1932, when they were called Brigadmil or (Voluntary) Brigades of Militia. This organisation was not particularly active or effective, so in 1959 the Central Comittee of the Communist Party and the Council of Ministries established the Peoples' Voluntary Druzhin or DND, specifically to help tackle rising hooliganism and alcoholism.

The brassard and two kinds of small membership badges were worn by unit members on civilian clothes - they wore no uniform. The small medal on the left was awarded to a volunteer with a fully trained dog

able to do various police tasks such as patrolling public events - football matches, national celebrations, or pop concerts.

(Bottom right) **Voluntary Militia membership card and breast badge, 1975.** The DND became more important in the 1970s-80s, as the growing post-war generations in large industrial cities caused increasing problems for the authorities. These teenagers started to listen to rock and later punk music, established their own bands and gangs, consumed remarkable quantities of alcohol, and followed Western fashions in clothing and hairstyles - the favourite features being long hair and black market Western or even Hungarian-made jeans. While some of this so-called Soviet 'hippy' or 'beat' generation became famous artists or musicians, most of them were simply destructive, rebellious enemies of public order.

Besides the brassard and the badge a DND membership card was issued so that voluntary agents could identify themselves. Note the new kind of hairstyle sported even by the holder of this card.

(Above) **Militia Special Medical Service.** In May 1969 a special Militia unit was set up to deal with the chronic problem of public alcoholism, collecting up drunks and transporting them to hospitals. After medical treatment offenders were often sentenced to do public works, usually cleaning the streets in the early mornings with a police escort. The latter had various easily cleanable blue or black working uniforms. Their 20cm wide brassard bore the legend 'Special Medical Service' in yellow. Initially they had no cap badge, but in 1971 one was designed (second row, second left) with no police symbols but a prominent red cross.

(Left) **MVD cap & breast badges:**
Breast badges: National Bank Security Guard (left) and Traffic Police (right).
Cap badges (first row): Prosecutors, second version, introduced between 1954 and 1956; Militia officers, parade, from 1969; Militarised Guardsman, from 1982.
(Second row): Special Medical Service from 1971; Militia commanders, and Militia cadets everyday, from 1965 in silver, from 1977 in gold.
(Third row): Militarised Guardsman, between 1969 and 1982; Militia commanders from 1947 in brass, after 1956 in aluminium; female Militia headgear, male pilotka, and OMON combat cap.

MVD Militarised Guards

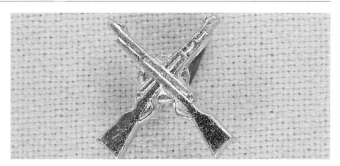

A special branch of the Ministry of the Interior (earlier, of the NKVD) guarded strategically important bases, industrial sites, power stations, special convoys, sometimes bridges, administrative centres, stores of goods or gasoline, and other large state properties. This organisation was termed *Voyennizirovannaya Okhrana*, VOHR - Militarised or Armed Guard. Their uniform changed often, but some general attributes which identify them are that they used various shades of green as a distinguishing colour, and an emblem of crossed rifles, usually with fixed bayonets, which was first seen on their green-painted cap badge in 1934. The rifles appeared on cap badges, collar patches, and in the 1930s-40s even on buttons behind the usual star but without the hammer-and-sickle. Their white metal or silver-painted belt buckle with the bayoneted rifles is extremely rare, and is often described wrongly e.g. as a snipers' or early Tsarist period buckle. In fact the buckle was produced for a short period only after 1951, when the Soviet Army also introduced the brass star buckle for enlisted ranks and sergeants. The VOHR usually did not wear rank badges or shoulderboards; if they did display rank badges these were worn on collar patches in the pre-1943 style of geometric forms in plain metal finish. Forest Militarised Guardsmen had similar cap badges with a green-painted background (see opposite page, bottom). Guards of commercial ports had more naval-style uniforms with a cap badge of embroidered crossed rifles and an anchor.

(Below left) VOHR collar patch. The patch was always green, and this shade of green was used only by Okhrana *personnel - it differs from the Frontier Guards colour. Note that the shape of the patch worn on the* gymnastiorka *is similar to those worn on coats before 1943. Rank badges were very rarely used, and then in the pre-1943 system of miniature triangles, squares, bars, etc, in a horizontal row beneath the crossed rifles emblem. They bore no coloured enamel, showing a plain brass or later aluminium surface.*

(Below right) Militarised Guardsman, early 1950s. This guard has the old-style 'square'-visored cap with a khaki top and green band and piping. The small star cap badge is supported by the crossed rifles, and the round base resembles that of the generals' cap badge between 1940 and 1955. His gymnastiorka *is of the old design with a fall collar, probably made before 1942 and left over from wartime stocks. VOHR personnel in the post-war years were usually retired Militia or Army officers serving in less dangerous locations - as here, at a* Kolkhoz *(collective farm) store and park for heavy machinery and fuel.*

(Top left) VOHR visored cap, 1970. *The cap badge was introduced from 1969 'for servicemen guarding the sites of the People's Economy'. Note the small size of the visor. The unusual colour combination of this cap has made its identification difficult for many collectors, especially when it is found with incorrect badges; to add to the confusion, it was produced with regular Army side buttons.*

(Left) VOHR pilotka, 1982. *Note that this is of the same colours as the visored cap above - green piping on dark blue material. This piece displays the later M1982 two-piece badge. All kinds of MVD and KGB troops and any ranking personnel preferred the more prestigious visored cap, so MVD or KGB pilotkas are rarely found.*

(Above) VOHR cap badge. *This Okhrana cap badge (left) was designed in 1967, and is very similar to the Army officers' cockade (see right) but without the hammer-and-sickle. The cockade was intended for issue to high and medium rank commanders, but in fact remained a prototype and was never issued to service personnel. These kinds of abortive insignia are obviously very rare because of the small quantities made. Collectors have to develop an instinct for distinguishing original pieces from irregular examples made for the commercial market. Some helpful points are the factory stamps on the back, the materials used, the method of attaching the different parts together, colours, and the paints used.*

(Left) VOHR buckle and badges. *The buckle (bottom right) is the same size as the Army or Navy enlisted ranks' pattern but usually in silver colour. This is one of the clearest examples for collectors of the many speculative identifications which can arise from a lack of knowledge of the true origin and date of a piece of militaria. (Top left) is an 'On Duty' breast badge. Note the design on the rare aluminium buttons (bottom centre). The cap badge with green centre and oakleaf wreath (top right) is for command personnel of Forest Guardsmen of the VOHR under the control of the MVD. (See insignia of other forestry organisations on page 129.)*

Internal Forces

Internal Forces (VV) were MVD troops fulfilling the same internal security funtions after 1946 as had the NKVD before the end of World War II. Their staff included career professionals but, as with the Frontier Guards, most of the total strength was provided by two-year conscripts. Uniform and insignia were similar to those of the Soviet Army. Specialist clothing was issued to limited numbers of VV special units analogous to those of the Ministry of Defence, e.g. armoured troops, flying and seagoing crew, laboratory personnel and chemical protection units; working uniform was issued for duty in garages, harbours, etc. These kinds of *specodezhda* (special clothing) were also similar to Ministry of Defence issue (see *Book 1*), but with MVD insignia. Their insignia were dominated by the brick red colour which gradually but totally replaced the dark blue NKVD distinguishing colour. Dark blue became the exclusive colour of the KGB (see relevant chapter below).

It should be mentioned that prison guards were also part of the Internal Security troops and wore uniforms with VV distinctions.

(Left) Badge 'For Excellent Service', 1962. After the structural changes in 1962 many badges were issued with new abbreviations; in place of 'NKVD' or later 'MVD' the legend was now 'VV MOOP'- Ministry for Protection of Public Order. This badge was awarded to MOOP Internal Forces enlisted personnel. It still includes the remains of the traditional dark blue colour of State Security. Note the shield shape and the Kremlin tower.

(Below) Unit commander and soldiers, c.1970. Internal Forces and Frontier Guards enlisted men were, like Soviet Army troops, conscripts fulfilling their two years' compulsory military service. Their uniforms were the same as those of the Army except for the colour of the insignia (shoulderboards, collar patches and sleeve patches); the only difference was that on summer field uniforms they used full colour shoulderboards with yellow letters ('VV', or 'PV' for Frontier Guards), while Army troops in field uniform had khaki shoulderboards without cyphers. Their basic training was also similar to that of Ministry of Defence troops.

This lieutenant-colonel wears the new-style M1969 combat uniform with khaki insignia (khaki shoulderboards and stars, collar patches, emblems, buttons, cap badge), and the ribbons of his mostly wartime medals; the only difference from an Army officer's field uniform is the brick red colour of the stripes on his shoulderboards. The soldiers have the summer everyday/field uniform (these were the same, since they used the everyday shoulderboards on field uniforms too), with brick-coloured collar patches (here with the driver emblem) and shoulderboards with 'BB' (Cyrillic 'VV') for 'Internal Forces of the Ministry of Internal Affairs of the USSR' - Vnutrenniye Voyska, MVD.

Note the universal GAZ-69 vehicle used for various purposes - as a command, radio, MP or medical car. Unusually for a command vehicle, this example mounts a grenade launcher. Later this vehicle was gradually replaced with the UAZ-469.

INTERNAL FORCES VISORED CAPS:

(Top left) Enlisted ranks', walking-out uniform, mid-1960s. Khaki top, dull 'brick' red band and piping with star badge; black chin strap.

(Centre left) Officers', mid-1960s. Similar to enlisted mens' but still with the dark blue piping as a reminder of the earlier NKVD dark blue crown. Later this piping also became brick red.

(Bottom left) Officers', field, M1958. All khaki apart from brick red piping. This was the same in the Internal Forces and Army. It was also issued for generals with branch piping. It was used first with the gymnastiorka *and later with the M1969 officers' field jacket.*

(Below) Badge 'For Excellent Service', 1968. This later version of the Internal Forces enlisted ranks' award was designed and issued in the year when MOOP reverted to its former name, so the legend is once more 'VV MVD'. Dark red is now dominant as the colour of the new VV insignia. It is unique in that the legend 'For Excellent Service' appears on the reverse side of the shield-shaped award.

CAREER SERGEANT, INTERNAL FORCES PRISON SERVICE, EVERYDAY UNIFORM, 1980S

Throughout the Soviet forces, while conscript sergeants who attained that rank during the term of their obligatory military service wore similar uniforms to the junior enlisted ranks, career sergeants - i.e. those who re-enlisted voluntarily after completing their compulsory service - wore smarter uniforms more similar to those of officers. The most significant similarity was the cut of the collar and arrangement of the patches, which differentiated officers from junior enlisted ranks in all the Soviet armed services. For officers and professional NCOs - as here - the lower edge of the collar was angled upwards and outwards, and the lowest point of the collar patch was on the inner edge of the collar. For junior ranks - e.g. see page 100 - the lower edge of the collar was angled downwards, and the lowest point of the patch was on the outer edge.

Career NCOs also wore the officers' cap badge and belt kit; however, except for the parade uniform cap they always wore the black chin strap of the junior ranks on their visored caps. Another distinction of career servicemen was the absence of characters - the initials of the Soviet Army, Frontier Guards, Internal Forces, Fleets, etc. - from the outer ends of their shoulderboards.

This NCO provides a good example of a career sergeant, wearing officers' style tunic and cap badge. His cap distinctions and collar patches are in the dull brick red which was for many years the basic distinguishing colour of Internal Forces. The rank stripes on his shoulderboards are also dark red instead of Army yellow.

FEMALE COLONEL, INTERNAL FORCES PRISON SERVICE, PARADE UNIFORM, 1986

This female prison commandant has the 'wave green' parade uniform with skirt, and brick red cuff piping and collar patches; the gold shoulderboards also have two brick red lengthways rank stripes beneath the three stars. Colonels' winter headgear was similar to that of generals, but without the red top. Because the male equivalent of this hat was called the papaha, *this female version was nicknamed the* mamaha. *The officers' parade cap badge with the wider, ornamented cockade was used only on parade visored caps; on this hat she wears the smaller wreathed cap badge originally issued to Air Force and paratroop officers, but adopted during the 1960s-70s for parade style headgear by officers of all the armed services. The parade uniform was always worn with black shoes or black boots, while brown shoes were worn with officers' everyday uniforms.*

On the right breast she wears the Excellent Service award, and on the left note her 10 Years' Service Medal; this indicates that she has no more than 14 years' service at this date - another year would bring her the 15 Years' Service Medal.

(Right) Collar patches for walking-out uniform. (Left to right): KGB in so-called 'cornflower blue', with general service emblem; Internal Forces in 'brick red', general service emblem; Militia in bright red, Militia coat of arms emblem; KGB Frontier Guards in green, general service emblem. Alternative speciality emblems included e.g. legal branch on Militia patches, or on the KGB, VV and Frontier Guard patches those for driver, medical, signals, or band. However, note that a brick red patch with the hammer and monkey wrench emblem identified the Ministry of Internal Affairs fire brigade units.

(Below) Some sleeve patches of security services enlisted ranks. (Top row): General service patches for the KGB, KGB Frontier Guards, and Internal Forces. (Second row): Cavalry units of the KGB, KGB Frontier Guards, and Internal Forces. While mounted cavalry had generally been relegated to ceremonial duties, the Frontier Guards still employed horsemen in areas of extreme terrain.

(Third row): Komandirovka (headquarters traffic control units) of KGB; Internal Forces from 1990; Internal Forces from 1992; Internal Forces Komandirovka.

Other known examples include dark blue with harp for KGB Kremlin Guard Band, embroidered for soldiers and with gold piping for officers, for the parade uniform worn on national holidays. Most of the regular specialty emblems were

theoretically issued on the Frontier Guards' green base, e.g. paratroops (see page 122), engineers, aircrew, signals, musicians, etc., though never apparently the 'K' for Komandirovka; but most personnel actually wore the general service sleeve patch with their specialty identified by the collar emblem.

(*Top right*) *Headquarters traffic control police helmet.* Like the Army, the KGB and Internal Forces also had Komandirovka headquarters traffic control MP units who enjoyed special authority for ensuring the rapid and secure movement of convoys. Various high visibility items were worn on duty, including a (usually self-painted) white helmet with a red star and stripe. The truncheon was always black-and-white, though some battery-powered luminous models were also issued.

(*Centre right*) *Academy student shoulderboards and year stripes, 1969-91.* (Left to right): Frontier Guards, and Internal Forces (extra long for wide shoulders), for everyday tunics; Militia summer parade (post-1979) for white shirts, and everyday (1969-79) for green shirts; KGB for everyday shirts. The Militia used metal characters, the others plastic. Note that the student's 'K' (for kursant) was introduced only after 1979; in 1943-79 the wide yellow side stripes on various types of shoulderboards were the only identification for training schools.

The cadet's academy course year was indicated by one to five yellow (earlier, sometimes white) 1cm x 7cm stripes (kursovski) on the left sleeve 1cm below the general service arm patch of his branch, on cloth backing of the appropriate colour (here, Internal Forces). A sixth stripe was added by final year students at the Military Medical Academy, whose six-year course brought officer rank and a medical doctor's degree.

(*Right*) *Medical officer's diploma, 1959.* The separate sheet lists the marks obtained on the most important courses. So what subjects should a doctor be familiar with? History of the Communist Party of the USSR; Political Economy; Historical and Dialectical Materialism; Scientific Communism, etc. The stamp at the top of the certificate confirms that a 'graduation badge was issued to the bearer'.

OFFICER, EVERYDAY UNIFORM, MID-1980s

This blouse-style uniform was widely used from the second part of the 1980s. It was popular for its improved comfort and ease of movement in contrast to the service tunic, and for its convenient breast pockets. Note that belts were not used over this blouse. When the holstered Makarov had to be carried on duty the belt - without its shoulder brace - was worn under the blouse.

This Internal Forces lieutenant's branch is identified by the brick red cap distinctions and rank stripes along his shoulderboards, his rank, by the stripes and stars on the boards; and his officer status, by the gold braid chin cords on his cap.

MAJOR-GENERAL, SUMMER EVERYDAY UNIFORM, MID-1980s

The shoulderboards are detachable. Note that in the Army, Air Force, KGB, Internal Forces and Frontier Guards, the white or green shoulderboards provided for wear with summer shirtsleeve order by generals and warrant officers had no branch-colour piping, so the branch of service could normally be identified only by the coloured distinctions and badges of the visored caps. The only exception was the Frontier Guards, where the green shirt was used with bright green warrant officers' shoulderboards instead of khaki (see the Frontier Guards warrant officers' shoulderboard on page 92).

(Below left) Enlisted ranks' winter ushanka. This type was also used by enlisted servicemen of the Army, Air Force, KGB and Frontier Guards.

(Below) Officers' pilotka. The summer uniform was worn with a visored cap and shoes when 'out of formation', and with the officers' pilotka - distinguished by branch-colour piping - and boots when 'in formation'.

INTERNAL FORCES HEADGEAR, EARLY 1980s:

(Top right) Generals' everyday cap.

(Centre right) Officers' everyday cap.

(Bottom right) Warrant officers' and career sergeants' cap; similar to the officers' version but with black chin strap.

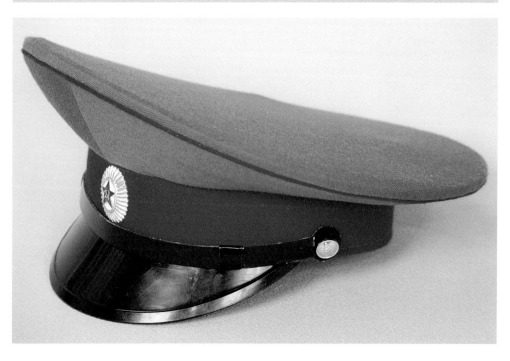

Spetznaz

The often loose use of this term in the past has caused a good deal of confusion; and before considering uniforms an explanation of its meaning, and its relevance to Ministry of the Interior troops, is in order.

'Spetznaz' is an abbreviation of 'Units for Special Missions'. In practice it refers to special forces units, a concept broadly similar to the elite troops of most other advanced military powers, e.g. the SAS and SBS in Britain, the Navy Seals and Airborne Special Forces in the USA, and many others. In the USSR their history can be traced back to the 1930s. Soviet Spetznaz were first seen on the battlefield during the Spanish Civil War, when they formed part of the military assistance sent by the USSR to help the Spanish Republic defend itself against General Franco's Nationalists and his German and Italian supporters. Later, during World War II, such units were formed to organise sabotage operations against the invading Nazis.

The modern Spetznaz were born in 1974, when the so-called 'Alpha Group' was organised, initially under the direct command of the KGB. Later the Ministry of Internal Affairs Special Forces were formed inside the MVD Internal Forces as a subordinate unit, at first in company strength. Their function was to fight against the internal enemies of the system. Other Spetznaz groups, trained and equipped for various missions behind enemy lines, were also formed under the command of the Ministry of Defence within the paratroop and naval infantry units. These latter did not display any recognisable sign of their special status on their regular paratrooper or naval infantry uniforms.

The Spetznaz of the Ministry of Defence and the other agencies were among the most carefully selected and best trained soldiers of the Cold War era, achieving exellent physical and mental standards. One of the entry requirements was knowledge of two Western languages. They learned to use every Soviet and Western hand weapon and heavy weapon system. The MVD Spetznaz was famous for its anti-terrorist tactics, especially against hostage-takers. These Internal Forces special units were committed both to the fight against organised crime, and against nationalist and separatist movements in the last years of the USSR, especially in the Baltic states and the Caucasian Republics.

(Above) Stetchkin automatic pistol. Produced in 1950, this weapon entered service the following year. Designed to give high firepower to officers and soldiers on especially dangerous combat service, the APS pistol took its name from its inventor, Igor Yakovlevich Stetchkin. Its magazines hold 20 rounds of the same 9.2mm ammunition as the Makarov, in a staggered row. It can be fired single-shot, or fully automatic at a theoretical rate of 750 rounds per minute; in practice, an experienced user can achieve about 90 shots per minute including three or four magazine changes. Its old-style wooden (later bakelite) holster-stock can be fixed in the same way as that of the 'broomhandle' Mauser K96; with the shoulder stock fixed the effective range increases from 50 metres to 200 metres. Although it is no longer in general use in Russia, North Korean state security border guard officers still carry the Stetchkin.

(Right) Three faces of the city of Tula in badges. Tula, an ancient Russian town south of Moscow, has three different images. One comes from its centuries-long history as the site of Russia's largest weapons factories, which have produced everything from Cossack sabres to the various AK assault rifles. Tula was also named as a Hero City, the most respected award for courageous endurance during the long fight against the German invaders in World War II. Finally, Tula is also known for a factory producing samovars, the traditional Russian tea urns. There is an old joke that a retiring master craftsman is presented with one piece from their parts of the production line by each of his colleagues. A week later one of them asks him if he has suc-

ceeded in assembling his samovar yet. He answers that however he tries fitting the parts together, the result always comes out as an AK47...

(Below) The maker's stamp on a 1953-made Stetchkin APS. The shield with star was another mark used by the Tula weapons factory. The APS was made for use in heavy combat, but it failed because of its high weight of almost 2kg (4.4lbs), and its extremely bulky holsters and magazine pouches. During exercises it was found that some soldiers could not leave armoured vehicles quickly and safely because of the encumbering size and shape of the holster and its shoulder strap.

(Below) Internalisation of external parts. The unwieldy size of the Stetchkin, and the unpopularity of impractical uniforms, prompted Soviet designers of the early 1980s to devise a generation of more comfortable and functional combat uniforms with concealed buttons, pockets for weapons and munitions, and improved freedom of movement for the users. Here an armoured vehicle crewman's overall has a special breast pocket to take the Makarov pistol.

(Right) Paratroopers' padded helmet, 1984. *Spetznaz paratroopers used similar equipment to regular Ministry of Defence airborne troops, but often enjoyed priority for the issue of the latest items. This headgear was one of the latest models in the final years of the USSR. Similar to the tank crews' protective helmet but without integral communications gear, it was always made in this khaki-green colour. It was often retained after a parachute jump, and was sometimes worn for ground operations not necessarily involving air insertion. The heavy padding gave some protection against injury during urban or hand-to-hand fighting, which was one of the specialities of Spetznaz training.*

The Soviet system, involving central planning and procurement but widely dispersed manufacture and often inefficient distribution, caused two simultaneous problems for the armed forces. There were persistent shortages of some items, especially personal items such as cleaning materials (every serviceman had to wash his own clothes), cigarettes, quality food, and communication and transport items. Yet there were sometimes incredible surpluses of other items, which continued to be issued and used, or exported, up to half a century after their first production.

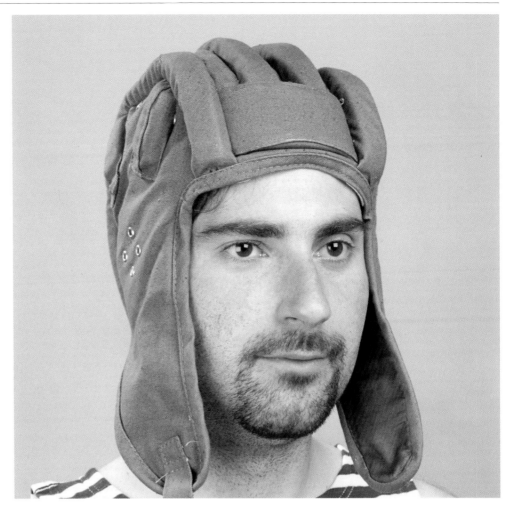

(Right) Spetznaz beret for officers, 1989. *The MVD Spetznaz beret was 'brick' red, like all Internal Forces uniform and insignia distinctions. Issued only to fully trained and qualified Spetznaz personnel, it was introduced in 1989 as the first visible uniform feature identifying the Spetznaz. Although most of the unit members had paratrooper qualifications, and many of the officers had previously served with para units, officers nevertheless wore the Army ground troops style of badge cockade, not the Air Force airborne officers' cockade with ornamentation around the oval star badge. (Ministry of Defence and KGB Frontier Guard para officers always wore the Air Force style cockade.) Spetznaz officers, like other Internal Forces officers, trained and studied in both MVD and Army academies.*

(Left) Camouflage patterns, one-piece clothing. *Various colour combinations of the one-piece KLMK camouflage overalls are illustrated here. It was produced in different colours and with spots of different shapes and sizes; the earlier models had rounded, the later, square-edged spots. Note the two differently shaped and coloured face masks. Although rare, such masks were issued as early as the 1920s. The image of a mask also appeared in the collar emblem of the camouflage engineers (who designed and built hidden bunkers, etc.) and camoflage units (which concealed e.g. camps, artillery pieces, tanks, etc.) in 1922 and later in 1924.*

(Left) The inside surface. *The one-piece KLMK camouflage overall had another pattern on the reverse surface; this was especially useful by night, reducing the visual image of the sharp silhouette of the moving body when seen through infra-red vision devices. (From the Tibor Pirisi collection)*

(Right) Colour variations, two-piece clothing. Five colour variations of the more coarsely-woven two-piece camouflage uniform are visible here. Originally they were designed for use in different climatic areas and different configurations of terrain and vegetation - e.g. the lighter colours for tropical areas with minimal vegetation, the darker green for evergreen coniferous woodland, etc. In actual service they were used as and when they were available, however, and sometimes even with the top and bottom halves of the suit in different patterns.

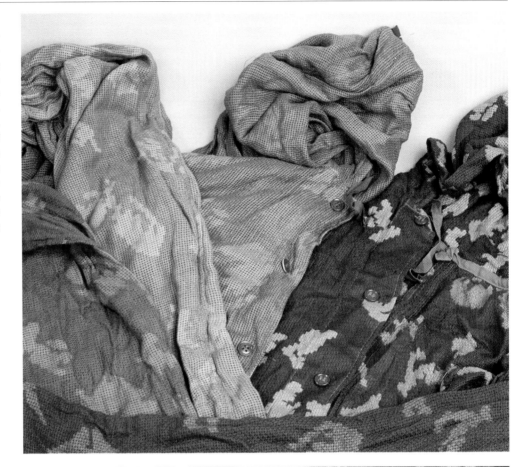

(Right) Labels on two-piece camouflage uniforms. Between 1979 and 1989 markings were stamped on large cloth labels of different colours. It is rare to find them in used pieces, since they often protruded from the inside, and the first thing any soldier in Afghanistan did when receiving this issue was to tear off the labels - especially the highly visible white and blue ones. The colour of the label was supposed to indicate the terrain or climate where that garment was recommended for use - white for desert areas, green for temperate areas with normal vegetation, and blue for humid forest with darker vegetation. Note that these examples were all made in the same city, Gukovo. The labels carry the same data as stamps on other military clothing - e.g. on the white label here the name of the clothing company, size 2 (medium), issue year 1979, and in the small acceptance 'box' of the military quality controller, his number 69 and the quality 'first class'. Similar small stamps are often found inside the synthetic lining of visored caps. Most Soviet military marks are stamped directly onto the cloth, and are often found on the inside of the internal parts of the lower pockets.

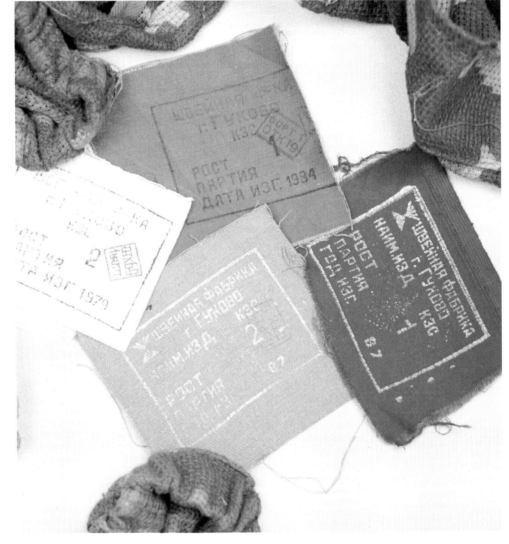

SPETZNAZ SOLDIER, 1988

(Above) *This MVD soldier somewhere in the region of the border with Afghanistan is working with strengthened KGB Frontier Guard patrols to prevent the penetration of Afghan guerrillas into Soviet territory shortly before the final withdrawal of Soviet troops from Afghanistan. He wears the latest summer camouflage modification of the M1982 afghanka type combat uniform, with a combat cap instead of the beret. He has the combat belt system with suspenders, green-painted buckle and grenade pouch. His weapon is the rechargable RPG18, the final version of the RPG grenade launcher family. The telescopic tube weighs only 2.5kg (5.5lbs), and can be made ready for launching is eight seconds. Designed for use against armoured vehicles but valuable in other combat scenarios, the RPG18 has an effective range of 200 metres. The bag pack at his feet carries five more of its 64mm rounds. The general issue protective goggles were often used by vehicle crews or with RPGs and shoulder-launched anti-aircraft weapons such as the Strela. Just visible is his Poljot (Pilot) wrist chronograph/watch produced for the armed forces. (Photo by the late Gyula Jászberényi)*

SPETZNAZ TRAINEE, 1989

(Right and opposite) *In the USSR, as in many other countries' armies, to wear the colourful beret of an elite unit was a privilege marking a man as a selected and fully trained specialist, who had passed a punishing physical training course and had acquired all the necessary skills for his role. Soldiers still undergoing training and assessment who had not yet passed their final tests wore a much simpler heagear. In the case of the Spetznaz this was khaki, the same colour as the field uniform; the badge worn on it was a subdued khaki-green star of the same size as that for the pilotka.*

This Internal Forces conscript, who has volunteered for special duties, wears a two-piece camouflage suit of one of the palest patterns, over the blue and white striped undershirt of elite units. The small pouch on his belt is for two 'corn' grenades (the Russian nickname for 'pineapple' fragmentation grenades). The AK bayonet could not be fixed to his RPK weapon because of its longer modified barrel with attached bipod, but was still carried, since it was extremely useful in hand-to-hand combat.

(Above) **RPK with its canvas carrying case.** *The RPK was designed by M.T.Kalashnikov; it was originally made - from 1955 - in 7.62mm, and from 1974, when the USSR changed its standard small arms calibre, in 5.45mm. There is also a folding stock version, and drum magazines are available in place of the curved box magazines.*

Mikhail Timofeyevich Kalashnikov

As one of the most successful arms designers in history, whose weapons - either complete or de-activated - are legally collectable in some countries, Kalashnikov perhaps deserves a little space here. He was born in 1919 in a small village, the 17th child of a peasant family. He worked as a technician for the Turkestan-Siberian Railway. In the Army he was a tank technician and driver in the Kiev Military District from 1938, and contributed various technical innovations for tanks. During combat service as a tank

commander he was seriously wounded in 1941. Invalided home, he started to develop a sub-machine gun in the workshop of his railway depot. After showing the prototype to Party and Army authorities and ballistic experts his potential was recognised; he was sent to an artillery academy, and then to the Central Research and Development Testing Centre of the Red Army. He worked on several weapons, before finalising the design of his fully automatic assault rifle. After modifications the weapon was tested in 1947; the results were outstanding. He had created what is arguably the most widely known, reliable and effective personal firearm in history - the AK47. Various versions have been used and/or manufactured in more than a hundred countries; and Kalashnikov's design principles have been copied by manufacturers not only across the former Communist world but also in Finland, India, Egypt and Israel.

Kalashnikov went on to develop a standardised series of firearms with similar operating systems, interchangeable parts and similar ammunition, at first in 7.62mm and later in 5.45mm calibre. The simple original design has acquired folding stocks, grenade launchers, folding bipods, various bayonets (see *Book 1*), silencers, and optics; it has been shortened, water-proofed, civilianised for hunters, and even curved. It has been produced with wooden and plastic stocks (it is alleged that the finishing treatment of the original wooden stocks proved irresistible to voracious termites in some tropical countries).

Kalashnikov's weapons are relatively cheap and simple; in properly trained hands they are very effective, and adequately accurate to all practical battle ranges; they are robust, easily cleaned, and reliable in all climatic conditions - in other words, more or less 'soldier-

proof the world over, which is probably their most significant advantage over the competition.

Kalashnikov became the chief firearms designer of the Soviet Army and received several awards, e.g. the Stalin and Lenin Prizes, three Orders of Lenin, two awards of Hero of Socialist Labour, a doctorate of Technical Sciences and the rank of general. At the time of writing he is still working. Given the popularity of his invention in many post-colonial Third World countries, he can boast the unique distinction of having depictions of his rifle incorporated in the national flags, coats of arms, or military awards of a number of sovereign nations.

(Right) **MVD Spetznaz instructor.** *He wears the KLMK one-piece camouflage overall* (kamuflirovanniy letniy maskirovochniy kombinezon) *and the brick red beret, and is using a rangefinder periscope.*

(Left) Spetznaz trainee with instructor. *Teamwork, and the mutual trust which comes only from taking responsibility for comrades in small groups, were among the foundations of the highly effective performance of the Spetznaz units.*

(Below) Spetznaz sleeve patches, c.1992. *The USSR passed into history in December 1991. These two insignia were made the following year as distinguishing patches for Spetznaz - the first time such insignia had been seen. It is interesting to note that they still used the red star of the former Communist system rather than the tricolour of the new Russian state. The motif of a shortened version of the 5.45mm AK74 with folded stock recalls a typical weapon of the special forces; the fist symbolises superior skills in hand-to-hand fighting.*

(Lef) **The rear of the combat belt system.** *Because Spetznaz units were usually employed for violent but short-duration missions, e.g. hostage rescue, attacks on terrorists or criminal gangs, etc., they typically carried minimal equipment on the belt and Y-straps. Shovels, rain capes/ tent sections, etc., were not attached. The two large slung canvas carriers are for the periscope and the RPK. Note the hoods of the camouflage jacket and suit.*

(Right) **Detail of the shoulder brace.** *The sling of a weapon or backpack can be attached to the Y-strap of the belt system.*

Fire Brigades

The national fire service came under the control of the MVD; but throughout the vast territory of the USSR there were many fire-fighting organisations linked to practically every human activity. Neighbourhood communities, factories, the transport system - all had voluntary fire brigades, or at least members trained in fire-fighting. For instance, every large railway station had a red-painted fire train with water tanks, tool wagons, and personnel on 24-hour duty, sometimes with a heavy crane wagon. Areas of obvious hazard also had fire protection teams, e.g. airfields, military bases, nuclear power stations, fuel depots and chemical factories; there was also a forest fire service. These might be under direct MVD control, or detached or voluntary groups financed by the appropriate company or other organisation. The latter had various uniforms and protective gear.

(*Opposite left*) *Fire service medals.* These are two of the most common awards to firemen, both instituted in 1957. The medal 'For Bravery in Fire' (left) showed a fireman rescuing a child from a burning building. Most of the recipients had saved lives or 'Socialist property' in fires or explosions. The reverse bore the name of the medal and a crossed axe and monkey wrench. The medal 'For Saving Life' (right) was awarded to firemen, military personnel, members of life-saving organisations, and to private citizens of the USSR or other countries who selflessly risked their own lives to save others. A famous recipient was S.Karapetyan, a world champion underwater swimmer, who saved the lives of 20 bus passengers after an accident at an Armenian lake. The youngest holder of the medal was Pavel Kolosov, a 13-year-old Siberian boy, who received it twice. The obverse shows a swimmer rescuing a child; the reverse bears a palm, hammer-and-sickle and star.

(*Opposite centre left*) *Fire service sleeve patches.* The brick red colour identifies the organisation as under MVD control. It is not known exactly by what dated order the badge was introduced. Note the darkening of the earlier example; the yellow plastic material fades in a matter of hours in bright sunlight.

(*Opposite centre right*) *Excellent Fireman badge.* This was instituted in 1944, at a time when more than 20 similarly styled badges were introduced for 'excellent' armed forces personnel (e.g. submariner, sniper, scout, mortarman, artilleryman, and even Army baker, cook, and pontoon bridge builder). These were originally made of brass with enamel finish. Later they were unified into just three patterns, one each for the Army, Fleet and Air Force. The fire brigade variant survived this rationalisation, and 'Excellent Fireman' badges were still issued in the 1970s, though now - like the one illustrated - made from aluminium.

(*Opposite bottom left and right*) *Badges for visored caps.* (Left) Voluntary Fireman, 1974. The abbreviation is for 'All-Russian (the old-fashioned name for the Russian Soviet Federal Republic) Voluntary Fire-Protection

Association'. The Ukrainian Association had a different pattern. (Right) MVD fire service enlisted ranks, 1964; a silver-coloured version is also known.

(*Right, top and centre*) *Fire brigade helmet, 1955.* This steel helmet was originally issued to militarised fire brigade personnel, but was widely used by all kinds of fire-fighting organisation from 1955. The badge features a fire engine with rising ladder beneath a star, flanked by a hammer, monkey wrench and fire hoses.

(*Below*) *Painted helmet.* The badge has lost its importance on the white-painted helmet, and has been overpainted with the number '7' to identify its user. White items were normally used for parade purposes in the armed forces (e.g. belts, hats, tunics, gloves), but here the colour and number are simply to give maximum visibility e.g. in heavy smoke. The original green colour shows on the edges and damaged areas.

Civil Defence

This embraces both military and state security organisations. Among the first civil defence teams were the Local Air Defence Units. These were responsible for dealing with air raids; they built air raid shelters, kept public order, co-ordinated the efforts of fire and medical services, and secured important buildings. In 1940 the NKVD took over this organisation from the Red Army, and held it until 1960 when it passed to the Ministry of Defence. That ministry reorganised it and renamed in 1961 as Civil Defence.

(Top right) Rank badges. These were worn on both lower sleeves, normally in the form of one or two red stars. They can be seen being worn in documentary film footage of the Chernobyl nuclear plant disaster.

(Below) Civil Defence items, early 1980s. Large first aid bag with its contents; direction signs for use in disaster areas - WC, and First Aid Location; sleeve patch - note the medical branch emblem, common throughout the services, and the MVD brick red background. The red booklet is the 'Certificate for Blood Donors of the USSR'.

(Right) Sleeve patches. (Left) as used on everyday and parade uniforms; (right) water-resistant version as used on working uniforms and shirts. The Cyrillic 'GO' stands for Civil Defence.

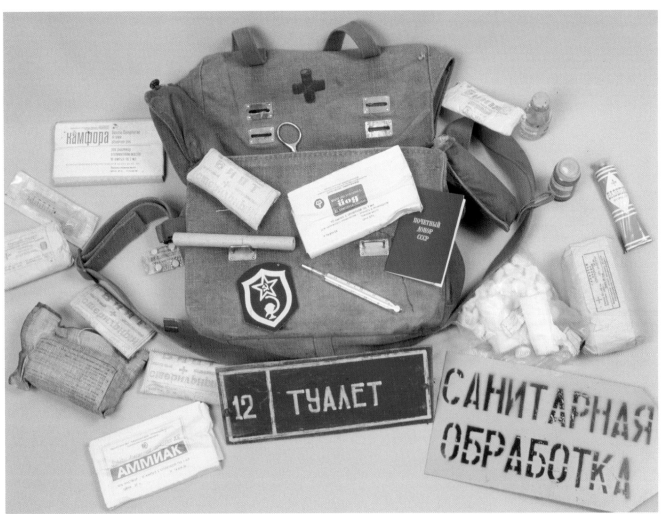

(Right) Special gasmask for children. During the Cold War large numbers of gasmasks were produced in different sizes to fit all ages of children. This piece from the mid-1950s had technical similarities to contemporary military patterns; however, the filter is smaller and lighter, and the mask is easier to fit, covering the face only and leaving the top of the head free. Here it is worn by a Pioneer, *a member of the school-age Party youth organisation. Pioneers were recognisable by the red tie and white shirt, and sometimes wore a* pilotka *style hat.*

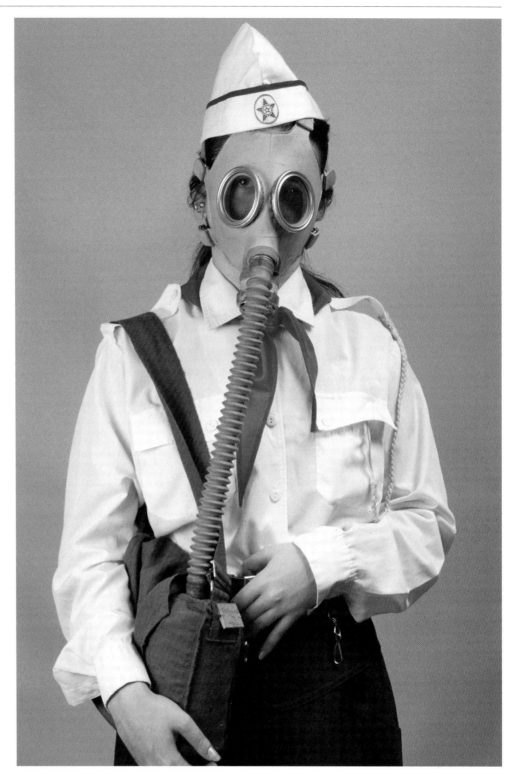

(Below left) Breast badges, from 1968: 'Ready for Civil Defence of the USSR', *and* 'Excellent Civil Defence Worker'.

(Below right) Blood donors' badges. For the first, second and third donations; the first two were issued in 1964, the third is a later edition.

(Right) **Civil Defence gasmask.** *Note that the eyes were unprotected, but it has two filters for better respiration.*

(Below) **Chemical Defence items.** *Gasmask with its bag; chemical sample collecting kit; and sleeve patches of the Civil and Chemical Defence organisations, which worked closely together at every level.*

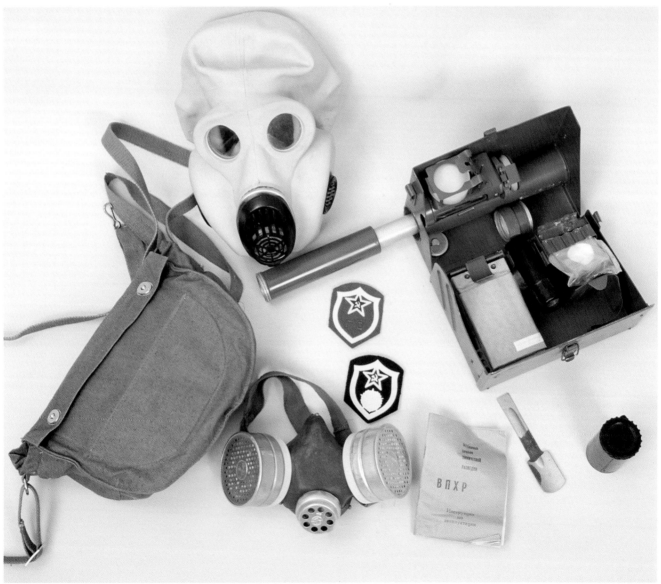

Court Personnel

(Right) Prosecutor, 1958. Until the 1950s court personnel also wore uniforms. From 1922 the lawyers of the Revolutionary Military Tribunal were identified by a sleeve patch. From 1943 even civil attorneys had uniforms, with shoulderboards and a shield emblem which was similar to the later prosecutor's cap badge (see page 55 bottom). After the death of Stalin in 1953, one visible sign of the move away from personal dictatorship was that prosecutors and lawyers - who had been compromised by their acquiescence in Stalin's gross abuses of the legal system - changed their uniform and rank insignia. The more civilian appearance of the clothing after 1954, without shoulderboards, symbolised that the court had abandoned its military trappings and character and become more a part of the civil service. The attorneys in military courts also wore this uniform.

The 10cm-long collar patches with two vertical stripes and one 25mm star shown in this picture identified State Prosecutors. This man worked in a court under the command of a city military commisariat.

(Below left) 50th Anniversary Badge of the Revolutionary Military Tribunal, 1968.

(Below right) Prosecuting attorney's collar patches, 1954. The grades of First, Second and Third Adviser to a State Prosecutor wore patches with a single stripe and three, two and one 20mm stars. These are the patches of a First Adviser.

KGB - Committee for State Security

In 1941 the NKVD was divided into two Committees: one for Internal Affairs, and one for State Security. From 1943 the NKGB (People's Committee for State Security) was separated completely from the NKVD (People's Committee for Internal Affairs). From 1946, like the other former committees, it was renamed as a ministry, the MGB (Ministry for State Security). For a short period after the death of Stalin in 1953 it was re-united with the MVD. It received its definitive title and position in the often-changing hierarchy on 13 March 1954, when it was named the Committee for State Security (*Komitet Gosudarstvennoy Bezopasnosti*, or KGB) and placed under the direct control of the Council of Ministries as part of the central *apparat*. The symbols of the KGB were the 'cornflower blue' distinctions on the uniform; the badge of a shield and sword; the mythical status accorded to Felix Dzerzhinsky, the founder of the state security service; and Lubianka Square, the headquarters of the KGB near the Moscow Kremlin.

(Below) MGB Lieutenant-Colonel, 1952. The white M1943 style kitel *was not often used by Army officers below the rank of general; and note that branch colour piping and lace collar bars were never used on this garment. The edge piping and rank stripes on his shoulderboards are dark blue. He wears medals for service in the Far East, that for the Liberation of Korea (see Book 1 page 59), a Mongolian and a Chinese medal - he probably served as an instructor or adviser in these countries.*

(Right) Breast badge, Excellent State Security Worker.

(Below right) KGB service book, 1956. The text on this old-format ID book shows the new privileged place of the organisation in the politico-military structure: 'USSR Military Book for Reserve Officer of the State Security Committee under the Council of Ministries'. Note that the most important ID documents are not always red.

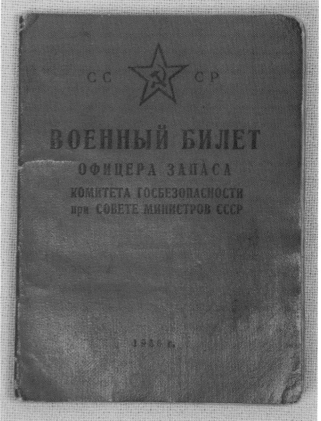

(Left) Officer's parade cap, 1955. Introduced with the new grey parade uniform designed for the tenth anniversary of the victory over Germany, this is the only cap with gold ornamentation on the visor ever made in the history of Soviet parade headgear. The grey parade dress was abandoned a few years later in favour of a more moderate khaki parade uniform. During this period the other armed services had similar caps with different colours and piping.

(Left) Officer's everyday cap, 1955. The first pattern of KGB officers' visored cap used with everyday uniforms, its khaki crown distinguished by dark blue piping and band. It bears here the M1955 officers' cockade. Note that at this date the crown is still relatively small, especially when compared with hats of the late 1980s.

(Below) Graduated KGB cadets with instructors, 1955. This is a photo taken to record the historic moment when cadets received their officers' shoulderboards. The cadets still have soldiers' field uniforms with enlisted ranks' M1951 belt with brass star buckle. Note the brand new parade shoulderboards with gold base, dark blue officers' stripe, and the wreathed star infantry (or in the KGB context, 'general service') branch emblem introduced in 1955. The sitting cadets at left and right already display senior lieutenant's and captain's rank respectively, as outstanding students; the others have graduated as lieutenants. The cadets are not noticeably youthful; all would have been experienced career NCOs before officer training. The instructors are the major sitting in the centre, and the balding captain standing second left; they wear the officers' belt. The major seems to have Internal Forces shoulderboards with lighter brick-coloured stripes. Militia, KGB and Internal Forces often studied in the same institutes or academies, especially in this early period; even in more recent years the MVD Academy had its Militia and Internal Forces faculties co-located.

(Above) Shoulderboard, Moscow Honour Guard Company, 1955. These shoulderboards were used by soldiers and NCOs from 1955 until 1962, while the Honour Guard was under Ministry of Defence control. The gold braid edging remained the sign of central parade units until the end of the Soviet era. The '1' is this Detached Company's number. Note the new infantry emblem introduced in 1955, replacing the former crossed rifles. The medium sized button is still brass but the emblem is already made from painted aluminium.

(Top right) Lieutenant, Kremlin Honour Guard, 1965. The Kremlin guard was under the command of both the Ministry of Defence and State Security at various times. The first revolutionary honour guard may be said to have paraded even before the October Revolution: when Lenin returned to Petrograd from his long years abroad on 3 April 1917, sailors guarded the Finland Railway Station and a military band played the Marseillaise and the Internationale. The first unit to welcome foreign delegations was established in 1941: the 120-strong 'First Guard of Honour Motorised Rifle Company of the First Battalion of the First Regiment of the Dzerzhinsky Division of the NKVD'. Their first 'guest' was Winston Churchill the following August. The most important post of the Honour Guard was at the Mavzalej (Mausoleum) of Lenin in Red Square; the special

drill performed when changing the guard was so fast and complex that it was difficult to follow with the eyes. Their uniform was as colourful and as well made as possible.

This junior officer wears a special ushanka made from Persian lamb, an expensive material regularly used only for the headgear of honour guards and of generals and marshals (the so-called papaha, see page 37). All ranks also wore the yellow embroidered officers' parade belt. Parade and Honour Guard formations retained the SKS45 Simonov semi-automatic rifle after the introduction of the AK47, as being more suitable for drill movements.

In 1962 the KGB took command of the Kremlin guard and established its Kremlin Detached Regiment. From that time onwards they used dark blue insignia, as seen on this officer's collar patches.

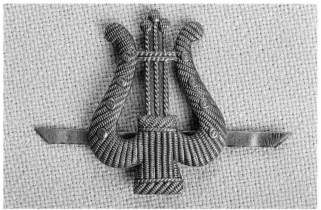

(Right) Cap badge M1955, Joint Military Band Regiment, Moscow Garrison. This brass badge was fixed onto the front crown of the visored cap above the usual cap badge, for all ranks. After this became a KGB unit the members also wore embroidered musician's sleeve patches on cornflower blue for both arms, with added gold piping for officers from the early 1970s.

(Right) The Honour Guard ushanka. Enlisted men of the Kremlin Guard also wore Persian lamb winter hats but with the enlisted ranks' cap badge. Note that the top is the same light blue-grey as the officers' parade greatcoat which the enlisted men wore at their Kremlin posts.

KGB COLONEL, 1956

A strange combination of everyday uniform items in a transitional period. The uniform (like all later KGB uniforms) is dominated by the dark 'cornflower' blue distinguishing colour of State Security. The old-fashioned kitel *is tailored with a fall collar, with M1955 collar patches and sewn-on shoulder-boards. The differences from the earlier M1943 tunic are the disappearance of the closed standing collar, and of officers' piping on the cuffs and collar; and the movement of the branch emblem from the shoulderboards to the collar patches. This is the last time that breast pockets would be seen on the tunic. The old-style cap officially received the new officers' cap badge, with its oval cockade, from 1955; so this is probably the last time the 'all-ranks' star would be seen on an officer's cap. Note his Service Book for career KGB officers.*

(Above) Unofficial badges. Some badges from the 1960s-70s, promoting the cult of Felix Dzerzhinsky (1877-1926), the first head of the Bolshevik Cheka in November 1917, and thus the founder of the Soviet state security service. A Pole born in Vilnius, Lithuania, who had once been attracted by the priesthood, Dzerzhinsky later harnessed his capacity for fanatical devotion to the Bolshevik cause. He spent many years tirelessly struggling against the Tsarist Okhrana secret police, and was imprisoned and tortured. He learned from his persecutors, and copied their methods when, from 1918, he became an implacable driving force behind the 'Red Terror'. His statue stood outside the KGB's Lubianka headquarters in Moscow; its removal was one of the great symbolic moments of the collapse of the USSR. After public discussion and a referendum, it has since been decided to re-erect it.

CAPTAIN, EVERYDAY UNIFORM, 1958

The cap bears the new M1955 officers' badge with its oval cockade; it has a black plastic chin strap - later officers wore gold chin cords on everyday as well as parade caps. The tunic is the new style introduced in this year, replacing the closed-collar version seen on page 87. As an everyday item it is simpler than the service tunic of the 1970s; the collar patches are not yet edged with gold. The shirt has a broad collar, as was the fashion at that time, and the tie is also wide. Note his everyday captains' shoulderboards with a blue rank stripe; these were made from the same material as the tunic, and followed the shape of the shoulders, in contrast to the rigid 1943 pattern.

Long service medals, from 1958. Each of the armed services had its own long service medals in three classes, but with slightly different characteristics. Around 25 different variations are known; besides the Ministry of Defence, KGB, MOOP, MVD, Internal Forces and Fire Brigade, their organisations in different Soviet Republics presented their own versions bearing different legends.

The KGB issue first version gave the number of years' service in Arabic numerals - '10', '15', '20' - as part of the legend on the reverse. The second version had Roman numerals - 'X', 'XV', 'XX' - on the obverse beneath the star. On the reverse the name of the organisation was not inscribed, but there was a small star above the legend. The first issues of the first class were struck in silver, the second class in cupronickel, and the third class in brass. (For comparison, see the Soviet Army version in Book 1, page 125.)

(Right top and centre) KGB first version, 1958-60 and 1968-91. *On the reverse the star is above the legend; the lettering is large; and the length of service is given in the legend in Arabic numerals.*

KGB second version, 1960-68. *On the reverse the star is below the legend; the lettering is smaller; and the length of service is shown on the obverse in Roman numerals.*

(Right) 20 Years' Service, MOOP. *The legends are MOOP + name of the Soviet Republic, 1962-66; MOOP + USSR, 1966-1968; MOOP alone, Ukraine.*

(Centre right) 15 Years' Service, MVD of Russian Soviet Federal Socialist Republic. *MVD + name of the Soviet Republic, 1960-62.*

(Far right) 15 Years' Service, MVD. *MVD + USSR, 1958-60 and 1968-91.*

KGB MILITARY ADVISER, CUBA, 1963

The military activities of the USSR and other Warsaw Pact nations (especially the German Democratic Republic) were focused not only on Europe; personnel were seen in many Soviet-oriented Third World countries. This KGB transport specialist is serving as an adviser in Cuba in the days of the famous 'Missile Crisis'. He wears an irregular combination of working/field garments: naval tropical shorts (partly because the other armed forces did not issue shorts, and partly because he is working with naval transport units); a tropical shirt with subdued shoulderboards bearing the transport branch emblem; and an old-styled panamka *tropical hat of the type introduced in World War II. Note his naval holster.*

(Below right) Tropical hat for naval personnel. With naval units making more frequent visits to tropical ports in the Third World, naval officers and advisers wearing naval uniforms received a new panamka *hat made from very light material in the colour of the naval everyday summer shirt. This example has a green (field) chin strap, a naval cap badge, and buttons dated 1957. It was first mentioned in the 1965 regulations, so it is possible either that earlier buttons were used from stock, or that the hat was already in use in the 1950s but that some detail change in the cut or material in 1965 led to its being mentioned again.*

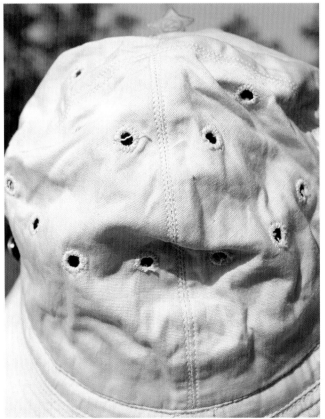

(Above) Orders and medals of an adviser. Note that awards were often given a few years after the events. All high-ranked awards were listed in a personal 'Book of Orders'.

This Far East expert first worked abroad in the Korean War, and received the Military Merit medal for Combat Service (the 'BN' abbreviation on the top line of his book means 'unnumbered'). He was awarded the Red Star Order for suffering a wound or injury, the Gold Star of Hero of the Soviet Union, and the Lenin Order. Note that Heroes of the Soviet Union almost automatically received the Lenin Order too; here their entries in his book are made with a single stamp, and they were both awarded on the 'Birthday of the Armed Forces'. (While the first Hero of the USSR award brought the recipient a Lenin Order, any second award brought the additional honour of having a bust or sculptural portrait erected in his home town or village.) In 1966 this man received the Red Banner Order for Vietnam War services.

To combat a perceived reduction in the value of the higher orders due to multiple awards, in 1988 the Supreme Soviet officially stopped the practice of presenting more then one Gold Star or Hero of Socialist Labour award to the same person.

(Left) Rear of the panamka.
In the back are two rows of ventilating holes; hats for officers were sometimes made with only one row.

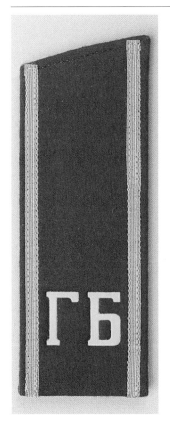

(Far left) KGB shoulderboard, Honour Guard, Lenin's Mausoleum, Moscow Kremlin. Like other Honour Guard units, the KGB Kremlin detachment had parade shoulderboards with narrow gold metallic thread edge stripes (not to be confused with the wider gold edging of cadets, e.g. p.63). In this late version the 'GB' (State Security) cypher is plastic; on earlier issues it was in metal letters.

(Left) KGB shoulderboards for enlisted ranks' everyday uniform of the Kremlin detachment. (Left) 1980s; (right), late 1991 - in the last days of the Soviet Union the 'GB' cypher of the unpopular KGB was replaced with 'OKP', for 'Detached Kommendatura (Kremlin) Regiment'. See also the earlier Kremlin guard shoulderboard on page 86.

Shoulderboards of KGB, Frontier Guards and Internal Forces.

These final patterns were introduced in the early 1980s and used until the end of the USSR. The sewn-on design with angled inner end was almost universal; the old 'hexagonal' shape with a removable button was retained only for shirt-sleeve order.

(Top row): Colonel, KGB, parade tunic; Lieutenant-Colonel, KGB, grey greatcoat; Captain, Frontier Guards, parade tunic; Lieutenant, Internal Forces, Transport troops, summer khaki-green shirt; Chief Warrant Officer, Frontier Guards, Mine Engineers, everyday khaki-green shirt (because no 'PV' cypher or green rank stripes appeared on warrant officers' shoulderboards, nor coloured collar patches on shirts, only the bright green base colour of the shoulderboards distinguished the user from Army troops).

(Second row): Yefreitor, KGB; Junior Sergeant, Internal Forces; Senior Sergeant, Frontier Guards (all three were used on parade, everyday and field uniforms, except summer shirts); and private, Internal Forces, general service, for everyday shirt.

**KGB CAPS, EARLY
1980s:**

(Top left) Generals' everyday, with gold embroidery flanking the cockade. Note the very high, large diameter crown typical of the period. On the generals' cap badge the ground behind the star is gold, on the officers' version, white-painted.

(Top right) Officers' parade. Note that the 'wave green' base colour used with 'cornflower blue' band and piping gives a noticeably different colour effect than with e.g. brick red distinctions.

(Centre left) Officers' everyday. Extended service sergeants wore a similar cap but with black chin strap.

(Centre right) NCOs' and enlisted ranks' parade and walking-out.

(Left) Generals' parade, late 1980s. This high quality cap, made to measure for the individual, has a high crown of large diameter, the all-gold badge cockade made in two pieces, and rich gold embroidery on the dark blue parts, on the chin strap and on the leather visor. The buttons bear the Soviet coat of arms.

FEMALE WARRANT OFFICER, 1972

This warrant officer (a rank introduced in 1972 throughout the armed forces) wears everyday uniform with 'on duty' or 'in service' accessories - the officers' belt with holstered Makarov pistol, the map case (here an NCOs' pattern), and the rolled officers' raincoat, plash-nakidka. *The uniform is basically the same as in field order but with yellow metal emblems on full-colour collar patches and yellow metal rank stars on the shoulderboards. The raincoat (shown unfolded in* Book 1 *page 92) was introduced by an order of 1954, but is first mentioned in the 1959 uniform regulations. Female everyday berets were khaki in all units.*

(Above) Tunic details. For NCOs' everyday uniform there was no gold edging around the coloured

collar patches. The shoulder brace of the belt was always worn passing under the right shoulderboard. Note the KGB breast badge.

(Above right) Rear of the equipment. By regulation the buckles of the straps should be in front, but to make movement easier in the field they were often arranged at the back. Note the water bottle and the strap carrier for the folded raincoat.

(Right) Map case. This could be worn either slung on its own strap, or as here, attached directly to the D-rings of the partupey *belt. This reduced the encumbrance of multiple straps worn over the shoulders, but made it more difficult to remove quickly.*

(Right) KGB officers' pilotka, **late 1980s.** *From the mid-1980s officers throughout the armed forces had a summer everyday uniform with a shirt worn outside the trousers (see page 64), used both with the visored cap, straight trousers and shoes when 'out of formation', and with the officers'* pilotka *and trousers tucked into boots when 'in formation'. The officers' khaki* pilotka *was piped in the appropriate colours, e.g. red for the Army, light blue for the Air Force, and dark blue as here for the KGB. The naval version was black with white piping (see page 117).*

(Below) Officers' pipings of the security services. *(Left to right): Frontier Guards, on parade tunic; Militia general, on trousers; Frontier Guards, on everyday trousers; Internal Forces, on trousers. Note that the 'cornflower blue' piping of the KGB was also used by Ministry of Defence cavalry units on their insignia, piping and hat; confirmed identification can only be made by reference to the sleeve patch or collar emblems.*

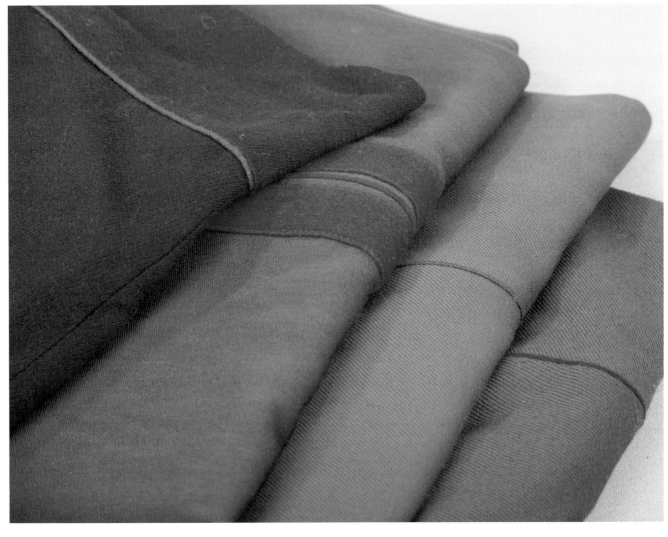

KGB Frontier Guards

The young KGB took over full responsibility for the frontier security of the USSR on 28 March 1957, and from this date Frontier Guards troops came under KGB command. The service's abbreviation of 'PV' (*pogranvoyska*) was retained, as was the long-established Frontier Guards tradition of green distinctive insignia, and especially their famous green-topped caps.

(Below) Frontier Guards awards. (Left) Excellent Serviceman of Frontier Guards, 2nd Class; the 1st Class was gold-coloured on a red ribbon. These were awarded from 1969. (Centre) Section leader's badge, 1973.

(Right) Medal 'For Conspicious Service in Guarding the State Border of the USSR' - possibly the medal with the longest name in history. Instituted in 1950, it was subsequently issued to approximately 56,000 servicemen.

(Left) Frontier Guards officers' parade cap, M1955. This pattern of officers' parade cap was introduced for all armed services - with appropriate piping - for the tenth anniversary of the victory over Germany (Army and Air Force versions are illustrated in Book 1, pages 71 and 123; the KGB version in this book, page 85). While all other versions had a grey crown, that of the Frontier Guards had their unique green top. The band is black, the piping raspberry red. Note that the cockade and the ornaments are made from separate castings.

(Right) Army medical and veterinary officers' parade cap, M1955. For comparison - this has sometimes been confused with the Frontier Guards' version. The band is dark green and the crown is grey, with red piping. Officers of these two services in fact co-operated in the field, Frontier Guards personnel serving alongside veterinary and medical troops of the Army and controllers from the Ministry of Agriculture.

(Left) Frontier Guards officers' everyday cap, M1955. The plain star was replaced with the new oval cockade. The black chin strap was still used; in this period gold chin cords were worn only on parade caps.

(Right) Enlisted ranks' cap, mid-1960s. The old enamelled brass star was replaced by a painted aluminium version in the 1960s. Note the unusual position of the visor.

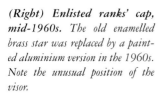

(Right) Frontier Guards officers' parade tunic, M1955. *The unique green-topped cap opposite was worn with this double-breasted grey parade tunic with open collar, piped green at the collar and cuffs. The 'trapezoid' gold lace shoulderboards with green stripes are sewn down. Regulations ordered the branch emblems to be moved from the shoulderboards to the collars for the first time since 1943 (see Book 1 page 71). This Frontier Guards officer, however, has moved his infantry (general service) emblems back to the shoulderboards - a rare and interesting example of this kind of irregularity in the highly standardised Soviet armed forces, though such details may sometimes be seen in original photographs or archive films. Another irregularity observed in this transitional period was that generals started to use the gold-edged red collar patches from their winter coat on the open-collar tunic, instead of the smaller oakleaf insignia worn without patches. Note also the cuff decoration.*

(Right) Long service chevrons for enlisted ranks, M1969. *Chevrons to mark the number of years a soldier had served were introduced from 1945 for enlisted ranks and sergeants who extended their service by contract (see the first version in the monochrome picture on page 27). After various changes, from June 1969 these stripes were introduced for Ministry of Defence troops as gold V-chevrons on backing of the branch colour. A few months later, in November, the KGB also introduced them, on green for Frontier Guards troops and dark blue for KGB units. They were placed 7cm above the cuff of the left sleeve. Both previously and subsequently service chevrons were used on all kinds of uniform, but in this period they were limited to parade uniforms. The 13mm broad stripes indicated five years, the 6mm, one year; e.g. the left hand (Army) set illustrated here is for 19 years (3x5 years, plus 4x1 year), and the right hand (KGB Frontier Guards) set is for 20 years (4x5 years).*

In practice these chevrons were not very often displayed. If a long-service veteran wore them on parade his comrades tended to call him a 'makaroni' man, after the numerous stripes.

(Below left) Post-war city medals. *The three largest cities awarded medals to deserving inhabitants who had lived for at least five years in Moscow or Leningrad or ten years in Kiev. The scope was very wide: recipients included citizens who distinguished themselves in the fields of industry, transport, economy, trade and development; in scientific, social and cultural life; workers in political, youth and trades union organisations; health and education workers; members of the armed forces, retired and invalid servicemen and workers; even deserving housewives. World War II defenders and partisans from these cities also received the medals. They were established on anniversaries of the foundation of the cities; illustrated here are (left to right) the Moscow medal, from 1947 (800th anniversary); Kiev medal, from 1982 (1500th anniversary); and Leningrad medal, from 1957 (250th anniversary).*

Lieutenant-Colonel's parade tunic, 1970. Despite immediate appearances, this is not a dark blue but a 'wave green' tunic; the effect is partly produced by the juxtaposition of the bright green Frontier Guards piping. This example has some archaic features: the wartime injury stripes on the right breast (here, for two serious wounds); the early brass M1955 collar patch emblems; and, most surprising of all, the smaller World War II American-made Lend Lease brass buttons with hammer-and-sickle motif (see Book 1, page 31), and smaller button-holes to match.

SERGEANT-MAJOR, c.1975

As a 'Unit Sergeant-Major on Duty' he wears the parade/walk-ing-out uniform. Usually non-career sergeants and men on various official duties wore the white belt (but sometimes the everyday brown one) with the AK74 bayonet on the left side. Note the old-style metal

'PV' cyphers on his shoulderboards. His badges are: Excellent Soldier (this Army format was also used by Frontier Guards units); next to it, Soldier Sportsman 1st Class, estab-lished in 1973 in red for 1st, blue for 2nd Class. Below these is the badge of a Section Leader of Frontier troops, also introduced in 1973 (see detail page 97). On his left breast is pinned his Komsomol (Communist Party youth organisa-tion) membership badge.

From 1974 service stripes for enlisted ranks were introduced throughout the armed forces (see Book 1 page 87). These straight horizontal stripes were worn on the right sleeve (both sleeves in parade dress, and sometimes irregularly on the left sleeve) below the branch emblem - one stripe during the first year of service, two during the sec-ond. In 1982 they were abolished by the Ministry of Defence, Ministry of Internal Affairs and KGB, because they were felt to encourage the endemic practice of the older soldiers bullying the new conscripts.

SERGEANT, 1959

Over field uniform he wears a one-piece winter camouflage overall, one of the early designs of the post-war period. The belt kit was worn over the camouflage suit; this belt and suspender arrangement, with various subdued belt buckles, was already in use during the 1950s. Even in winter and with field equipment the Frontier Guards' distinctive visored cap was worn. His weapon is the 7.62mm RPD section light machine gun; also designed by Degtyarev, this entered service in 1953, gradually replacing his earlier DP design. It is a belt-fed weapon, but the belt was often rolled inside a drum-shaped carrier to protect the linked rounds from dirt (in this configuration the gunner did not need a 'No.2' to feed the belt). When longer belts were assembeld the drum could not be used.

POUCHES:

(Top) Machine gunners had a round pouch for the RPD drum; it was similar to earlier PPSh sub-machine gun magazine pouches but larger, and often had a small extra pocket for an oil bottle.

(Centre) Riflemen carried the SKS45 Simonov semi-automatic rifle with pouches on both sides of the belt for the 10-cartridge straight-row chargers. Note also the canteen and carrier.

(Bottom left) Machine gunners additionally carried a grenade pouch. On such items soldiers often fixed a wooden name tag. Later, when issued with the AK47, riflemen too carried one magazine pouch and one for grenades on the other side.

(Bottom right) An alternative was to carry RPD drums in pouches slung from a shoulder strap. Here one is pictured together with the canvas protective carrier for an RPD. Note the small pocket on the side of the drum pouch, for an oil container.

MAJOR, FRONTIER GUARDS ADVISER, BERLIN, 1977

While most of the activities of the Frontier Guards were focused on the borders of the USSR, they were sometimes seen on other parts of the Iron Curtain as advisers or trainers for the local border authorities. This was especially true in 'hot' areas such as the Berlin Wall - from its construction in 1961, the best known symbol of the isolation of the two political systems.

This woman medical officer wears the M1976 female summer field/combat uniform - a kitel worn with a skirt - as used throughout the armed forces. It is a so-called 'peacetime' version; the stars on the shoulderboards, the branch emblems on the khaki field collar patches, and the officers' cap badge on the summer beret are all khaki-green, but the brass buttons are still shining, thus rather negating any camouflage effect. She holds part of the field laboratory kit for collecting, storing and analysing test samples from goods, liquids, foodstuffs and vehicles seeking to cross the border. Her Makarov pistol is secured to the belt by an extra lanyard strap. Note behind her the West Berlin rail carriages beyond the double defence line - first barbed wire, then a brick wall.

Health and veterinary personnel and quarantine inspectors under the control of other organisations - each with their own uniforms and insignia - also co-operated with Frontier Guards units: personnel of the Ministry of Agriculture, Water Resources Inspectorate, Border Quarantine Service, Ministry of Foreign Trade, Department of Exported Goods, etc.

(Inset) Winter hat for female officers, M1976. *This resembles the* papaha, *but is made from synthetic fur, and the wool top lacks the braid cross. In the 1970s the parade cap badge was the same as the later Air Force officers' everyday pattern, but - as clearly seen here - assembled from two separate pieces. There was a tendency to use this badge on the winter hat everyday or even field uniforms with female personnel. Note the field quality collar patches with medical/veterinary emblem, and the field shoulderboards with green stripes.*

FRONTIER GUARDS OFFICER, AFGHAN BORDER, 1982

Frontier troops were among the first units involved in the war in Afghanistan, and saw continued border fighting with several tribes long after the official end of the failed 'Internationalist Mission'.

This is one of the earliest prototypes of the new generation afghanka combat uniforms which appeared from 1982, in Frontier Guards camouflage pattern. Some features would later disappear as a result of practical combat experience: the buttons are not yet concealed, and are black instead of the later green; the breast pockets are divided into two - to take Makarov magazines - for officers only; and the skirt pockets have a single central button. The shoulderboards - from the material of the jacket, or sewn-on versions - are not yet used, so officer status can be inferred only from the magazine pockets, the officers' cap badge and leather belt. The panamka hat was rarely seen worn by officers, and is clear evidence that this officer is located in an extremely hot region. Panamkas of the Afghan War period in Frontier Guards camouflage pattern are more difficult to find than khaki or paratroopers' camouflage versions.

(Top right) Engineer Colonel, Frontier Guards, 1988. He wears high on his right breast the Order for Service to the Motherland in the Armed Forces of the USSR. Note the positions of his decorations. The basic rule was that decorations suspended from ribbons were worn on the left breast; on the right were displayed pin-on awards - i.e. high orders - plus all other pin-on insignia - e.g. academy badges, the Guards unit badge, wings, para jump badges, specialist badges, etc. As an engineer (identified by the branch emblem on his collar patches) he has the civilian silver Medal of Labour Heroism.

(Right) Order 'For Service to the Motherland in the Armed Forces of the USSR'. This was issued in three classes; here we see the 2nd (partly gold-painted) and 3rd (silver) classes - the 1st Class is entirely gold-painted. Instituted in 1974 and awarded from the 30th Anniversary of the end of World War II in 1975, it is the only large

sized post-war order without a ribbon. The symbols on it are the motor rifles (infantry) collar emblem for the Army, Frontier Guards and Internal Forces; an anchor for the Fleet; wings for the Air Force; and - as a novelty - crossed rockets for space research and missile troops. It was awarded for 'high effectiveness in military and political training of troops, for inventing modern military technology, excellent service, special command performance, bravery in combat, or other ways of serving the Motherland in the armed forces'. Most of the recipients were Afghan War veteran officers.

Benefits for the recipient included high quality living accomodation; one free first class train ticket every year, and all local and regional transport free (except for taxis); one free holiday or health care treatment in a special sanatorium every year; access to exclusive shopping and services (e.g. theatre tickets, or the top floor of GUM, the state department store next to the Kremlin, where only 'The Chosen Ones' could shop); a 15 per cent raise in retirement pension benefits; and privileged entry to university for the recipients' children. Such privileges were also enjoyed by the recipients of other high orders.

(Centre right) Reverse. The decoration was made from three pieces of silver fixed together with a screw, which also served to fasten it to the uniform. The stamp of the Moscow Mint was applied at the top, and the individual serial number at the bottom.

YEFREITOR, FRONTIER CHECKPOINT, c.1985

This private first class on duty at a border post wears the summer every-day shirt uniform introduced in the mid-1980s. Shirts were never embellished with badges or sleeve patches of any kind, and only shoul-derboards showed the branch and rank. This soldier has added old-type metal Frontier Guards cyphers to his green shoulderboards - a typi-cal touch for a smart man who took pride in his uniform. The characters are slightly smaller on the shirts' shoulderboards than on those made for wear with tunics. In 'adminis-trative service' a belt was not worn. Note the Soviet passport and the stamp which he holds. His cap is the usual green-crowned pattern of his service; this kind of green shade was also adopted for their distinctions by the border guard services in all Warsaw Pact countries.

(Right) The coat of arms of the USSR. These heavy stainless steel plates, measuring 20x22cm, were fixed to the border markers - red-and-green striped wooden or iron-banded cement columns - all the way around the 22.4 million square kilometre territory (twice as big as Europe) of the 15 Republics of the Soviet Union. The east-west extent of the country was more than 10,000km (6,200 miles) contain-ing 11 time zones. The length of its borders with a total of 12 neigh-bouring countries was more than 60,000km (37,280 miles) - one and a half times the circumference of the Earth.

MAJOR-GENERAL, SUMMER PARADE DRESS, 1988

In tropical areas parade uniforms comprised shirtsleeve order with tie, trousers and visored cap. For everyday tropical uniform a short-sleeved shirt was worn without a tie. This general officer commanding a section of the Soviet-Chinese Frontier District wears a white shirt with detachable white shoulderboards - introduced in 1972 for parade dress in hot areas - with the single embroidered star of his rank. The buttons on the shoulderboards and on the lavishly decorated parade cap bear the coat of arms of the USSR, as was usual for generals throughout the armed services. Note the non-regulation tie clasp, a Chinese Peoples' Army pattern bearing the portrait of Mao Tse-tung. This kind of irregularity was impossible in Moscow, but was tolerated in the remote Far Eastern corner of the empire.

(Below left) Protective headgear, 1986. *This padded fabric helmet, intended to protect the head and back of the neck and minimise heat loss, was used by Army and Frontier Guards personnel patrolling in conditions of extreme cold. Its shape allows the comfortable wearing of the* steel helmet over the top. It was such a rare issue item that its function is explained in a label stamped inside: 'Protective hat for territories of climatic zones No.I and No. II' - i.e. the Polar region. On Soviet uniform items the only instructions usually found are advice on cleaning and ironing. (This, in contrast to the instructions marked in some US garments, which treat the soldier as an infant child - e.g. on a US hat - 'Do not remove this label... If you feel cold in this hat, use a warmer hat... ')

(Below) An irregular example of the Frontier Guards sleeve patch. *This enlisted man has neatly added his service location (the border with Finland, 'Suomi' in Finnish) and the dates of his service ('1989-1991'). Note that he has not used Cyrillic lettering but the more fashionable Western alphabet, and the English acronym 'USSR' rather than 'CCCP'. An interesting direction for enlarging a collection is to seek out such non-regulation and individually modified items which give information about their owner or maker. It would also be interesting to track down irregularities in the uniforms of Soviet Army troops serving abroad, e.g. the use by officers of other countries' rank stars on their shoulderboards.*

LIEUTENANT, FINNISH FRONTIER DISTRICT, SUMMER 1983

She wears the M1983 female officer's everyday uniform with khaki beret, officers' belt and skirt. Interestingly, the left and right collar patches are irregularly reversed, placed as on enlisted ranks' uniforms and earlier field uniforms for officers. The uniform is almost the same as the preceding model but has gold-edged collar patches, previously used only on parade uniforms. Dark brown shoes were used with this summer order of dress. Her badges are a diamond-shaped academy graduation badge (this blue version is from 1970), and below it the badge commemorating the 60th anniversary of the Frontier Guards in 1978; on the left she sports the Finnish-Soviet Frontier Guards badge of the Kalevala District (see page 110). Note her 60x60 long range portable telescope; in perfect conditions this may allow her to recognize individual faces from distances up to 20km (12.5 miles).

FRONTIER GUARDS BADGES:

(Opposite top left) 60th Anniversary, KGB Frontier Guards of the USSR (1978), Murmansk District Checkpoint ('KPP' stands for 'checkpoint'). Like most such badges, this includes the red and green of the border marker columns.

(Opposite top right) 60th Anniversary badge, Nebit-Dagskiy District; both this and the Murmansk badge include an anchor motif, showing that there were also naval Frontier units in these districts.

(Opposite lower left) Heroes of the Frontier Guards, 1941-1971 - commemorative badge with motif of crossed Mosin rifle and DP machine gun.

(Opposite lower right) 70th Anniversary of a Frontier Guard district, 1922-1992. This badge was issued just a few weeks after the official end of the USSR, but its design still shows Soviet symbolism - the KGB sword, Soviet coat of arms, star, red flags, and an abbreviation of 'Red Banner Order-Awarded Frontier Guards'.

(Right) *(Top row):* *60th Anniversary, Red Banner Order-Awarded Lake Baikal District; two badges commemorating 60th Anniversary of Soviet Frontier Guards, 1978.* *(Second row):* *50th Anniversary, Red Banner Order-Awarded Murmansk District, 1968; 60th Anniversary of Soviet Frontier Guards, 1978.*

(Below) *Kalevala District, Soviet/Finnish frontier - note Finnish and Soviet flags; 50th Anniversary, Moscow International Airport Frontier Guards District; Leningrad District; 60th Anniversry, Lake Baikal District.*

FRONTIER GUARDS CAPS, EARLY 1980s:

(Top) Generals', parade

(Middle) Officers', parade - the only armed forces parade hat of the period which has no 'wave green' parts, although the rest of the parade uniform was in that colour (see page 100).

(Bottom) Soldiers' and sergeants', parade amd walking-out. Frontier Guards enlisted personnel often wore these caps even with combat or camouflage uniforms. There was also a tendency to put full colour insignia onto Frontier Guards camouflage uniforms.

PRIVATE OF DISCIPLINARY UNIT, 1985

Like every other organisation in which conscripts served, the Frontier Guards had a penal unit for refractory soldiers. This former private first class (yefreitor) - note the marks left by his lost shoulder stripes - wears the M1982 afghanka summer combat uniform in the Frontier Guards camouflage pattern; the shades of the field cap and jacket differ slightly. The only insignia he has are the Komsomol membership badge on his left breast, and the subdued green paratrooper's collar emblems identifying him as a former member of a KGB Frontier Guards airborne unit. Neither the cap badge nor the belt were usually worn during the term of 'labour therapy'; in winter the ushanka hat was often worn with the smallest star. The extremely short hair is a sign of a new recruit or a soldier undergoing punishment.

(Below) Physical and Formal Training Regulations, 1987. These training instructions were issued for Army and Fleet use, but Internal Forces and Frontier Guards also used them for the conscript training period. For soldiers in disbats (Discipline Battalions) a longer part of their service term was spent in training and in labouring, e.g. on Kolkhoz collective farms.

KGB Frontier Guards Seagoing Units

A significant part of the state borders of the USSR coincided with bodies of water - the Atlantic and Pacific Oceans, Sea of Japan, Bering Strait, Barents Sea, Gulf of Finland, Baltic Sea, Black Sea, and Caspian Sea. Seagoing units were employed from the first days of the Soviet system to protect territorial waters and the Exclusive Economic Zone. Their history in fact goes back to Imperial times when the Frontier Guards and the Customs Service maintained a sizeable fleet, especially in the Baltic (the Baltic Sea Customs Cruiser Flotilla). In later times they were also responsible for guarding Soviet waters against the fishing fleets of other countries such as Japan, which had an aggressive fishing policy; in these duties seagoing Frontier units co-operated with Customs and Ministry of Fisheries inspectors.

(Right) Frontier Guards Academy on-duty breast badge. Although produced after the end of the Soviet Union this badge still shows traditional motifs: the border marker; the winged propeller, star and anchor symbolising the air, land and seagoing Frontier troops. The legend is 'On Duty - Academy'. The tendency to wear 'on-duty' breast badges became more marked from 1990, when they began to be sported by policemen walking their beat, and National Bank guards (see page 55). The Traffic Militia (GAI) had started wearing them from 1985, and Army patrol members in Moscow and Leningrad from as early as 1973. Other versions are known from different periods.

(Left) Frontier Guards flag and cap tally. Soviet naval flags came in three different basic colours, all bearing the red star and hammer-and-sickle on a white field. A flag with an all-white field, with a light blue horizontal stripe along the bottom edge, was flown by Ministry of Defence combat vessels. A dark blue field, with the star and hammer-and-sickle on a white first quarter edged at the bottom with light blue, identified non-combatant Ministry of Defence vessels, e.g. supply boats, the rescue diver service, hydrographic ships, etc. The same but with this green field identified KGB Frontier Guards seagoing units. The tally is the general service cap ribbon for such units; other versions are known with 'NKVD', 'MVD' or 'KGB' prefixes. Sailors and officers wore the same cap badges as their comrades in the Fleet.

STARSHINA, FRONTIER GUARDS PATROL BOAT, 1974

This senior rating, equivalent to a sergeant, wears winter everyday uniform without coat. The jumper is worn with bell-bottom trousers, black shoes, black leather belt with brass 'anchor' buckle, telniyashka *striped undershirt, and* bezkazirka *hat with white piping. He holds the KGB naval flag of his boat. Note the 'Excellent Frontier Guard' badge, established in 1969. The sailors' hat was worn with a medium sized star badge without surrounding ornamentation. It is rare, because in 1969 the larger cap badge with ornamentation was ordered instead. On e.g. winter hats the medium star was ordered retained until the 1974 regulations, and the larger version was forbidden.*

(Top right) Details of the jumper. *This 1st Category* starshina *has three gold rank stripes on the short shoulder tabs worn in place of shoulderboards on naval jumpers; note that these are outlined in the green piping identifying Frontier Guards sailors. The detachable collar, always with three white stripes round the edges, is fixed with three buttons. The red left sleeve patch identifies the department or specialty - here, electro-mechanical. The pin-on metal badge on the right breast identifies the highest ('Master') class of specialist ratings, in the 1954-style brass first version. While other conscripts served for two years, sailors enjoyed three years' free food and accomodation... This senior rating's third year service stripes are also mounted on a green cloth Frontier Guards base. Decorative irregularities include an extra third button on the cuffs; and an anchor badge added to the third year service patch - the anchor is of the type originally ordered for the shoulder tabs of* kursant *naval cadets.*

Cadets wore their year stripes on the left sleeve below the department patch; enlisted ranks officially wore them on the right sleeve as here, but this order was often ignored, and they may be seen on the left or both sleeves. The Chairman of the KGB abolished the service stripes for enlisted personnel on 27 November 1982. Irregular uniform and insignia practices were more common in small units - such as patrol boat crews - where the conscripts were more isolated.

(Right) Belt buckles. *Naval buckles were used on black leather belts; white naval* remen *belts were usually limited to schools or parade uniforms. The upper* blahi *buckle is an early type used by enlisted men of all the armed services; this example has been bent into a curve by its user. The third, highly irregular buckle was worn by a Frontier Guards sailor; he photographed his fast patrol boat and fixed the waterproofed picture onto a piece of brass. This was probably an affectation for use with his demobilisation uniform. Note that the leather 'keep' should be about four fingers' distance from the buckle; some smart sailors acquired two of them.*

SOME NAVAL HEADGEAR:

KGB Frontier Guards naval units wore the same range and types of headgear as Fleet units under the command of the Ministry of Defence. The green Frontier troops piping was used only on shoulder-boards; naval style headgear had the usual white piping.

(Top) Admirals' parade cap. Note that the visor is not made of the usual plastic but is of fine leather, with gold-embroidered ornamentation on the top and a soft wool lining on the underside. The metal anchor-and-star is also surrounded by gold-embroidered decoration; and the band is of expensive silk.

(Centre and below) Officers' parade caps, summer/tropical and winter. Both the white and black patterns have large visors with gold ornamentation. They appear to be individually tailor-made, following the trend in the second part of the 1970s and even more in the 1980s, for the extremely high front and very wide top of the crown.

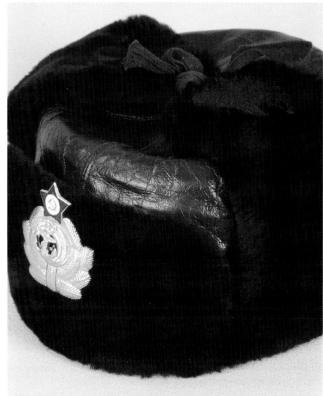

(Top left) Admirals' Persian lamb cold weather hat. *See the front of this hat in the photo at the top of page 119. Left inside 'used' head-gear, collectors may sometimes find interesting personal items. Even this admiral kept a basic sewing kit tucked behind the flap of his fine winter hat, for instant 'running repairs' to keep his uniform smart. Sometimes one finds cigarettes; money (sailors often hid a few dollars in their hats for use in foreign ports to purchase famous brands of cigarettes or drink); buttons; and rarely, in the liners of helmets used in actual combat in Afghanistan or earlier conflicts, the 'goodbye letters' which soldiers wrote to be sent to their families if they fell. An indication of the strong bond between soldiers from the same republics is the fact that these letters often mention how many soldiers in the unit are from the soldier's homeland.*

(Top right) Officers' leather-topped ushanka. *When the earflaps are down the entire outer surface is leather-covered and water-resistant.*

(Above) Sailors' ushanka. *The large wreathed star finally replaced the former medium sized plain star in 1974.*

(Right) Officers' everyday pilot-ka. *Note that this officer's cap badge has been bent into a curve to follow the shape of the* pilotka. *The cap was black with white piping for the seagoing Frontier Guards, like that of other naval units. Khaki caps with appropriate branch-coloured piping were issued in the other armed services (e.g. Army, Air Force, Internal Forces, Frontier Guards land units, VOHR and KGB – see in relevant chapters and in* Book 1*).*

KGB naval officers' items, c.1969. The background flag is the vimpel *swallow-tailed command pennant, flown from the highest point of a larger patrol boat serving as flagship for the 'Commander of the Convoy of United Frontier Guards Naval Units'. Note the shoulderboards of a captain first rank; the black base refers to the naval tradition, the green piping and rank stripes to the Frontier Guards distinctions. The captain first rank (equivalent to colonel) was entitled to a Persian lamb hat similar to those of naval generals and admirals (the rank of naval general was found in e.g. the engineer and shore defence branches). The old-fashioned TT pistol was still preferred by some officers; note its black naval holster. The brassard is for 'officer on duty at headquarters'.*

(Below) Mine specialist badge for seagoing personnel. This was given, from 1975, to reward outstanding long term service. A land forces version was also introduced in the same year, on a green ribbon; the design showed a soldier operating a mine detector on the obverse and newly built houses on the reverse.*

(Below right top) Stamp on reverse of Frontier Guards naval officer's shoulderboard. The bird with chevrons is the mark of the company which made shoulderboards and sleeve patches. 'COPT I' means 'Sort 1', or first class quality. The '15' stands for the length of the shoulderboard in* centimetres, and '1969' was the year of issue. The price at the officers' shop is given as '0 roubles, 90 kopeks'. Such purchases were subject to strict rules; the customer had to identify himself and show certificates proving his right to wear or simply to own the objects.*

(Below bottom) Seagoing Frontier Guards 50th Anniversary badge. A rare jubilee badge commemorating the organisation's half-centenary in 1968. Note the telltale green stripe on the naval flag.*

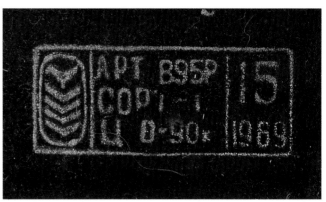

SEAMAN, FRONTIER GUARDS PATROL BOAT, 1969

This unlucky sailor has just ripped his coat sleeve on a ragged end of wire cable. This short coat or kurt-ka *is the only double-breasted uniform garment for enlisted ranks' everyday use in the history of the Soviet armed forces (Honour Guard parade uniforms sometimes featured double-breasted tunics). Its cut was unchanged since Tsarist times. Here it is worn with the black, green-piped shoulderboards, without cyphers, of the KGB Frontier Guards naval element. This coat is never worn with a belt over it. Usually it is worn with the sailors'* bezkazirka *('hat without visor'); in this case the cap tally reads 'Mine School Unit'.*

There has been some discussion as to whether enlisted men of this organisation used military or naval rank titles. Before 1946 in the Red Army the lowest ranking private was termed 'Red Army Man', of which the naval equivalent was 'Red Fleet Member' (Krasnofloteyets). From 1946 all land forces (Army, Air Force paratroopers, Frontier Guards, Internal Forces, KGB state security units, etc.) used Army-style ranks. Their manpower was based on conscripts, and the person without rank was called soldat *(soldier) or* ridovoy, *enlisted man (Militia ranks are given in the relevant chapter, above). Seagoing units of KGB Frontier Guards personnel used the same naval ranks as Ministry of Defence naval personnel, starting with sailor, then sailor first class, etc.*

(Inset) In cold weather sailors wore the black ushanka. *Note the green Frontier Guards piping around the black shoulderboards of the naval reefer coat.*

Details of naval binoculars. *The BM 7x50 pattern was introduced in 1968. They have large diameter lenses to give maximum visibility in all weathers; a shock-resistant structure with rubberised edges; and a water-resistant system. To keep the working parts dry, two small containers fit inside the body; these contain cobalt chloride crystals. This substance is hygroscopic, attracting to itself all moisture which penetrates inside the binoculars. As they become wet the blue crystals turn yellow or pink. Removing the containers and heating the crystals at 105 degrees C for 20 minutes drives out all the moisture, and the crystals can be replaced, to keep the binoculars dry again for months.*

KGB Frontier Guards Airmobile Division

AIRCREW OFFICER, EARLY 1960s

This helicopter pilot has an old fly-ing jacket dating from 1954, with a removable high-collared lining. Early jet crews had similar jackets before the issue of G-suits. Note the left chest pocket for a personal weapon. Some signs of modernity: the collar is already made from artifical fur, and the whole jacket uses no leather. The trousers (note the green officers' piping) are worn over brown shoes instead of tucked into the earlier boots. The visored cap already has the M1955 officers' badge mounted on an oval cockade, below added wings (see close-up). Airmobile troops of the Frontier Guards co-operated with the Ministry of Defence's Air Defence troops - 'PVO'.

(Below) Frontier Guards air-crew officers' visored cap. This was the regular officers' hat with added Air Force-style wings badge at the top of the crown. Note that the lower badge's cockade lacks the surrounding ornaments sported by Ministry of Defence pilots. Warrant officers always had a black chin strap, but from the mid-1980s onwards officers were allowed to wear a gold strap with everyday dress; the 1980 regulations still specify that the gold strap is only for parade caps.

FRONTIER GUARDS PARATROOPER, VITEBSK, JANUARY 1991

The paratroop units of the Frontier Guards airmobile division were stationed far from the borders, and from curious eyes, in hidden garrisons like Vitebsk in the Byelorussian Soviet Republic. Their function was to stay ready at all times to strengthen any border region of the Soviet Union within a few hours, in case of serious border conflict or incursions by any unwelcome visitors. They were usually transported by the helicopters of the small Frontier Guards air element.

Here we see one of the camouflaged versions of the winter afghanka uniform (see one of the summer versions on page 112). This camouflage pattern was preferred by Frontier Guards units but was also used by many other kinds of Army and paratroop units of the 1980s. As a member of the KGB Frontier Guards Airmobile Division he has a beret in Frontier Guards green with airborne insigia on the left side on a triangular pennant in the light blue of the Air Force paratroopers. At one time these elite troops were also issued a green-striped undershirt instead of the usual blue-striped pattern. He carries one of the various types of signal flare pistol in use; its large holster also contains a

number of rounds. Note above his left breast pocket the additional small pockets for five more flares.

(Inset) Sleeve patch. This was introduced from 1969, among various other KGB patches (see page 62); it bears the usual airborne troops emblem on green base colour.

(Above) Frontier Guards paratroop officers' parade beret. Frontier Guards officers with paratrooper qualfications were trained at the Kaliningrad and Moscow Higher Military Commanders' Schools of the Frontier Guards, and from 1976 onwards they wore this green beret with the blue side pennant and paratroops' branch emblem. For parade wear it bore the officers' parade cap badge with wide ornamentation flanking the cockade. For the Red Square parades they even put a metal inner frame into the beret to make it as flat as the top of a visored cap.

(Right) 50th Anniversary badge of the Vitebsk Airborne Guards Division. The issue date is not known. The unit was probably established as NKVD infantry or Army paratroopers long before the war. Note the Guard title and Guard stripes on the badge, which mean that the unit saw combat during World War II.

Training for hand-to-hand combat. In elite units an important element of the daily exercise was practising hand-to-hand combat with various weapons (here, the entrenching tool and AK bayonet). Note the uniform details: the large hood of the afghanka; trousers worn inside or outside the boots; the enlisted ranks' belt worn over the jacket, or in the loops of the long-waisted, warmly padded trousers (another, later version of the winter afghanka trousers were used with elasticated suspenders); and the green-striped telniyashka *undershirt.*

Customs Service

The Customs Service was a paramilitary organisation but under the control of the Ministry of Foreign Trade. The personnel of the service wore dark green everyday uniforms with special buttons bearing the coat of arms of the USSR on a shield (see photograph, right). The cap badge from 1987 was a version of the same symbol: the globe of the Earth, with hammer-and-sickle, was painted red, on a blue background, surrounded with oakleaves. At the top was a brass star, of the same size as a lieutenant's shoulderboard star; at the bottom was a rising sun with the Mercury sign, showing the connection to the Ministry of Foreign Trade.

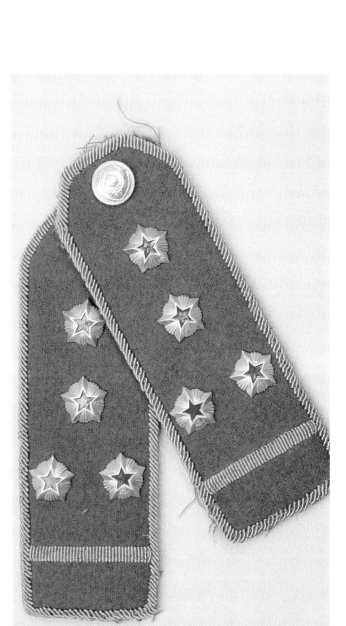

(Left) Captains' shoulderboards, c.mid-1980s. Customs Service shoulderboards have several special features. Since it was an all-officer service with no enlisted men, all rank distinctions were edged with gold piping. While all the other armed services had the officers' rank stripes on the shoulderboards lengthways (one for lieutenants and captains, two for majors and colonels), here the stripe is transverse, near the end of the shoulderboard. Note the especially handsome rank stars, with a 'cockade' background and red-enamelled centre.

(Above) Customs Service breast badge, obverse and reverse, 1987. Like the button motif and cap badge, the breast badge is also shield-shaped, with the coat of arms above the map of the USSR. The legend is 'State Customs Control'. The lower plaque - empty on this unissued example - is for the identification number of the bearer, usually in three digits. The reverse side shows the 'safety pin' fastening, also often found on other armed forces badges; and the stamp of the mint on the lower centre of the coat of arms.

Some political organisations

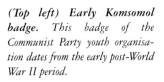

(Top left) Early Komsomol badge. *This badge of the Communist Party youth organisation dates from the early post-World War II period.*

(Above) Children's and Komsomol badges. *The first steps towards a Party membership card were taken almost as young as the first actual steps. The earliest political organisation, named after the October Revolution, worked in the elementary schools (the badge is based on the earliest known portrait photo of Lenin). As they progressed to the higher classes the pupils became members of the Pioneer organisation; and finally members of the Komsomol. They entered the Party only at the age of 25; in some of the monochrome portraits in this book servicemen of less than that age may be seen to wear the Komsomol badge with Lenin's portait. On military uniforms it was the only pin-on badge authorised to be worn on the left breast - over the heart.*

(Top right) Pioneer Congress delegate's badge, 1959. *Note the Sputniks, as symbols of modernity. The legend reads 'Second meeting (they chose this word because it also means 'flight') of the Pioneers, 1959'.*

(Right) Communist Party 50 year membership badge. *This miniature lapel badge - note the matchstick, for scale - copies the shape and colours of the Order of Lenin decoration, but with the number '50' in the centre; the legend on the flag is the abbreviation of 'Communist Party of the Soviet Union'. Given the horrendous losses during the Civil War of 1918-21, Stalin's massive purges in the 1930s, and the Great Patriotic War - and given the age of those who might qualify - not very many veterans lived to receive this award.*

(Left) Graduation badge of the University of Marxism and Leninism. This was the higher education institution for political personnel in the armed forces.

(Below) Communist Party membership book, 1976. This is the so-called Red Book. It was printed on one side in Russian and on the other side in the national language of the bearer. It is surrounded here by various badges, mostly with the portrait of Lenin, made to celebrate Communist Party Congresses. An interesting one to add to a collection would be that for the 20th ('XX') Party Congress in 1956, when in secret session the crimes of the Stalin era were officially acknowledged for the first time.

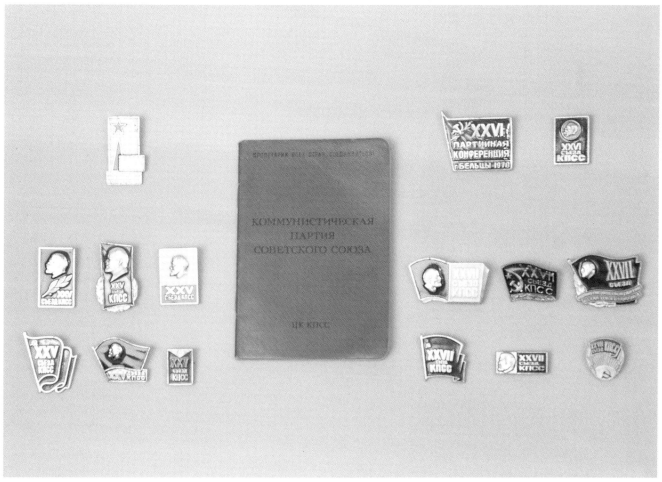

Membership identification, Supreme Soviet of the USSR. *This is for the ninth term, from 1974. Note the lapel badge. As previous party leaders had often appeared with rows of high decorations to which their claim was entirely political, President Gorbachev made a point of wearing only this badge, as a symbol of his legitimate power as an elected leader.*

Membership identification, Supreme Soviet of Uzbekistan. *This lieutenant-general was a member of the 'Highest Council' of the Soviet Republic of Uzbekistan in the 11th term, from 1985. Note the small additional card showing his status and confirming his right to privileges such as free airline tickets. (Incidentally, Kiev railway station still has a ticket window 'Only for Deputies of the Supreme Soviet' — but it seems to be less crowded these days.) The flag badge is in the Uzbek 'national' colours; officially each republic had its own flag and coat of arms, but in reality they were all similar to the symbols of the USSR - e.g. flags with red as the dominant colour, and the hammer-and-sickle featuring in the coat of arms. The portrait photograph makes it obvious that this general was of Russian rather than Uzbek ethnic background. The stationing of armed forces personnel far from their homelands was one of the reasons for the mixture of nationalities between the republics. Some other reasons for mobility were mass movement from small agricultural villages to distant cities in search of work and a better life; and further education, followed by employment and marriage, far from the original community.*

Other uniformed organisations

The last pages of this book are devoted to illustrating, for purposes of comparison and elimination, a selection of insignia associated with organisations which had no military or security role. It is often difficult for the collector or historian to identify unknown uniforms, caps, badges, collar patches, buttons, belt buckles, shoulderboards, etc., from the huge variety of uniformed groups which existed in the Soviet Union. Sometimes he will find unusual combinations of never previously encountered colours, piping and emblems. In the selection which follows, collectors should always note the critical points of difference from similar armed forces items.

It is impossible to describe here all kinds of Soviet uniforms; a whole book of similar size could be devoted to, e.g., the evolution of railway or merchant navy uniforms. It is impossible even to mention all the different organisations whose members are identifiable by their uniforms. The USSR was the largest country in history, and its uniforms differed in different areas and at different periods. Apart from the armed services which are our subject here, uniforms and insignia of sorts were worn by postmen, telegraphists, miners and lawyers; by personnel employed in all strands of the transport system - the riverine and maritime merchant navy, railways, airlines, bus and taxi services; by workers in schools, youth organisations and health services; by bandsmen, and by game wardens; by diplomats, especially in foreign missions; by hydrometeorologists, cartographers and nuclear power station engineers; even by undertakers (officially called Ritual Service Personnel, and unofficially 'Mourning Hussars'). The list could be extended almost indefinitely if we include the insignia of sports teams: every Warsaw Pact country had a privileged sports club for state security personnel, the names always beginning with 'D' - e.g. in Hungary, Dozsa; in Romania, Dinamo Bucuresti; and in the USSR, Dinamo Kiev.

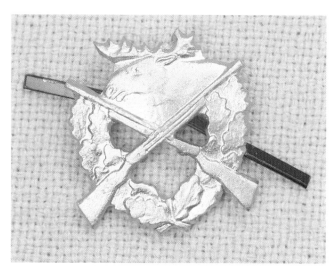

(Above) Sports club badges. Dinamo Kiev (here with the legend '12th Time USSR Champion, 1986') was the team of the MVD; TzSKA (Central Sports Club of the Army) was the team of the Ministry of Defence in Moscow. Thousands of designs of such badges are known.

(Above right) Officer's collar emblem, Forestry Service, 1985. Forestry workers had their own uniforms and badges from 1935. They had their own air service, too, who wore the Air Force wings on the crown of their visored caps.

(Right) Conservation official's breast badge, mid-1980s. This 'on-duty' badge was issued for Nature Protection Inspectors of the 'All-Russian Nature Protection Association'.

(Left) Forestry Industry sleeve patch, mid-1980s. The legend is 'Lesprom CCCP' - Soviet State Forestry Industry. The forests were a strategic resource, the property of the state and managed according to central planning.

(Left) Official, Central Apparat of the People's Committee of the River Fleet, 1941. The black cap, piped black, has a gold wreathed badge with a red pennant bearing the hammer-and-sickle. While sea- or rivergoing personnel had water-resistant painted metal flags on the badge, central and administrative personnel had this element embroidered. Note his double-breasted coat, without collar patches or shoulderboards; and, just visible under it, an old-style kitel tunic with standing collar. (We should recall that the Red Fleet was unique among the armed forces in retaining the Tsarist-style standing collar during the inter-war years.) The piping on the naval caps of services under command of the Ministry of Defence and the KGB was always white, but that of all other organisations, such as the merchant and fishing fleets, was black.

(Left) Fishing Fleet shoulder tabs. These were used (cf.KGB naval equivalent, p.115) on black (or dark blue) winter and everyday, and on white summer and parade jumpers, similar to naval jumpers. The legend reads 'Ministry of Fisheries'.

(Right) River Fleet specialists' wings and cap badges. The embroidered parade cap badge (top right) is for senior commanders, from 1969; a metal version was also made for everyday use (see picture below). The yellow plastic badge (bottom left) is for junior commanders. The same design was used on a white backing for home waters, and in silver on white for technical personnel. This black-backed yellow form was for junior commanders on foreign rivers, e.g. in Soviet boats on the Danube. Schools had a similar badge without the outer rim. This plastic type is a later version; previously it was made in metal like other cap badges.

(Below) River Fleet and Seagoing Fishing Fleet everyday cap badges, from the late 1960s. The badge with the pennant (left) was introduced in 1965 for junior commanders and kadets of the Seagoing Fishing Fleet. The triangular pennant on seagoing fisher- mens' and merchant sailors' cap badges goes back to the 1930s, when merchant and fishing sea and river fleets could be identified by different coloured pennants: e.g., light blue for Polar seas, red (with anchor) for the Caspian Sea, red (with hammer-and-sickle) for the River Fleet, red (with white star) for the Siberian rivers, and dark blue for Baltic Sea personnel. The badge with hammer-and-sickle (centre) is for senior commanders, that with a helmsman's wheel (right) for medium commanders of the River Fleet, both introduced in 1969.

(Above) Flight badge for 500,000 kilometres. Various badges were awarded to long-service civil pilots to mark their accumulated distances flown: for 300,000, 500,000, and 1,000,000 kilometres. The first version was made in 1935, and another in 1938, both with propeller aircraft; the later 1960 pattern featured a jet aircraft.

The badges were made from silver or sometimes from bronze; this example is the 1938 type in bronze. The 'GVF' abbreviation at the top stands for Civil Air Fleet; in practice this comprised only the single airline company Aeroflot. (The Air Force had no equivalent badges for accumulated time or distance in the air.)

(Below) Pilot's cap, Aeroflot, 1970. Note the upper badge of wings with the hammer-and-sickle. Ministry of Defence aircrew had the badge with a star replacing the hammer-and-sickle. Note the very large visor with metal ornaments.

(Above) Commander, Civil Air Fleet, 1940. Note his white summer hat with light blue piping; his collar patches with biplanes set against palm wreaths; and his parachutist's qualification badge. Officially he should wear an embroided wing with hammer-and-sickle above his command personnel cap badge, or, in an earlier version, a small hammer-and-sickle on the top part of the badge. The cap badge illustrated was introduced in 1940; the round central part is similar to an Army general's badge, but has a winged propeller superimposed.

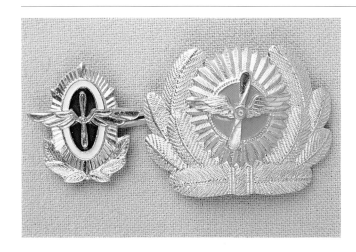

(Left) Cap badges, Aeroflot. *The smaller badge is for stewardesses (1977), the larger for pilots and command personnel (1965 issue).*

(Below) Pilots' and stewards' wings, Aeroflot. *The lower one with 'C' (the Cyrillic 'S') is for stewards.*

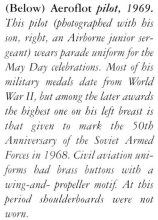

(Below) Aeroflot *pilot, 1969. This pilot (photographed with his son, right, an Airborne junior sergeant) wears parade uniform for the May Day celebrations. Most of his military medals date from World War II, but among the later awards the highest one on his left breast is that given to mark the 50th Anniversary of the Soviet Armed Forces in 1968. Civil aviation uniforms had brass buttons with a wing-and-propeller motif. At this period shoulderboards were not worn.*

(Far left) Crew badge, Magadan Airport in Eastern Siberia

(Left) Aeroflot *route and station badges.* *(Top to bottom):* North Polar routes badge - note the penguins and the aurora; Sachalinsk Airport in the Far East islands; Leningrad Pulkovo Aeroport.

Left) Aeroflot *emblem as used on shoulderboards.*

(Below) Aeroflot *aircrew badge.* This aircrew member badge was made by the Moscow Mint. For security reasons an individual number and the identity of the crew member are engraved on the reverse, just as on high medals and orders.

(Right) Air show badges. Participation in international air shows and exhibitions was a carefully planned aspect of Soviet propaganda from the 1930s onwards. These two badges made for French air shows feature the projected Buran Soviet space shuttle and its carrier, the giant Antonov An225, introduced to the public in 1989.

(Below) Veteran of the GVF badge. This was awarded for 30 years' service with the Civil Air Fleet.

(Centre right) Flag badge. This lapel badge features the flags of the Civil Air Fleet (Aeroflot), above the Soviet Air Force.

(Bottom) Aeroflot buttons. Early brass and later aluminium types.

(Above) Workers' Protection Inspectors' breast badges. These two examples from the 1970s identify inspectors in (left) an aircraft factory, and (right) a chemical plant. Their duties involved checking working conditions and safety measures, and trying to minimise the negative effects on the health of the workers.

(Right) Excellent Railway Worker badge, 1934. This badge was made in two versions, one in silver and one in bronze. Note that on the front of the locomotive is the name 'Stalin'. The two holes through the flag on this damaged piece show where a hammer-and-sickle was once mounted. Issued pieces were individually numbered on the reverse.

(Opposite bottom left) Excellent Railway Worker badge, 1978. The earlier image of the steam locomotive has been replaced by a diesel engine. Note the crossed hammer and monkey wrench at the bottom, and the Kremlin at top left. Again, the badge was always numbered on the back.

(Opposite bottom right) Railway workers' sleeve patches. These were issued from 1969. The left example is for junior grades, especially for conductors; the right, with a green rank chevron below, is for more senior grades, particularly engine driver *mashinists*. Note the combination of railway symbols - the winged wheel and the hammer and wrench. The abbreviation 'MPS' stands for Ministry of Transport Networks. Similar patches were issued for city subway drivers with the legend 'METRO' instead. Metropolitan transport (the underground train system) was administered separately from the rest of the major cities' public transport, since the Metro had strategic importance; it was the only part of the system which could function safely in wartime. The Metro tunnels were always connected to networks of secret passages and airtight bunkers for command and communication posts, water and food stores, militarised hospitals, and air raid shelters for tens of thousands of people in case of nuclear war.

(Left) Aeroflot *pilot, post-1943; & railway official, post-1943 (centre).* Both these military-style uniforms were introduced in 1943, the railway example on 13 September by order of the Peoples' Committee for Transport Systems (NKPS). Since civil aviation also came under the control of this ministry-equivalent, the same dated order probably covered Aeroflot uniform as well. Both uniforms are close copies of the M1943 standing-collar military tunic, with similar shoulderboards and rank systems. The pilot is a captain, with four stars on the shoulderboards. The railwayman, with one star, is a junior lieutenant equivalent - a 3rd or 4th class locomotive driver, or the brigadir *(team leader) of a repair crew.* Aeroflot *personnel were distinguished by light blue piping, the wings and hammer-and-sickle emblem, and the winged propeller on the buttons and cap badge; the railways, by green piping, a locomotive emblem, and a crossed hammer and wrench on the buttons and cap.

During wartime both civil aviation and the railways were completely militarised and put at the service of the war effort. They transported weapons, munitions, food and manpower towards the front; and evacuated factories, essential refugees and casualties on the way back, as elements of the planned military economy.

(Left) Railway worker, 1943. Note the railway personnel cap badge, issued from 1943: a crossed hammer and wrench, below a small star (similar to the one used on the soldiers' *pilotka* with a superimposed hammer-and-sickle). Between 1925 and 1943 railway personnel had larger star badges with the frontal image of a locomotive. Note that this man still has the pre-1943 falling-collar shirt, but the soldier on the right has the new gymnastiorka *with two-button standing collar. The legend on the sign reads 'Friends Forever'.*

(Right) Railway workers and railway police, c.1970. The workers have double-breasted jackets with winged wheel right breast and upper cap badges. Note that the man partly hidden in the centre background has an old-style crossed hammer and wrench cap badge, last issued in 1953. All these men wear civilian shoes; the issued protective boots were uncomfortable, and were usually traded or sold by the workers.

(Right) Female railway worker with railway policeman, mid-1960s. Between 1943 and 1953 railway uniform was similar to Army clothing, with a locomotive emblem on the shoulderboards and the crossed hammer and wrench on the buckle. After the ministerial reforms of September 1953 the uniform became more civilian in character, with open collars with black collar patches. The basic colours were black with green piping (especially on caps and patches). Only collar patches were used on shirts, which did not display sleeve patches. The head of the Ministry of Transport always wore a railway type uniform for ceremonial occasions, with a gold-based sleeve patch (with similar zig-zag embroidery to

that used for generals' shoulderboards) with a large embroidered gold star; above it was the coat of arms of the USSR.

Note the red-topped cap; and that instead of the regular protective shoes this woman wears warmer private boots of wool felt. Ranks were displayed on both sleeves; she is the 'Commander of Passenger Traffic' at her station, and wears a patch introduced in 1963. She has removed (or lost) the crossed hammer and wrench from the pentagonal patch, and one star is also missing from above the horizontal rank stripe. The top of the rank badge and the pentagonal patch are piped gold. Note also the Militiaman's belt buckle for enlisted ranks.

(Above) Railway commander (right foreground) with railway police, mid-1960s. The four stripes and four stars on the railway commander's M1963 sleeve patches indicate a very senior rank in the railway hierarchy - 'Divisional Commander of Goods Transport'. Note that while he wears the uniform of a civil organisation he still displays the ribbons of his wartime military service including the Victory over Germany and Bravery medals. On his right breast his hand partly hides the railway winged wheel badge; below it we can see the graduation badge of a technical or military/technical university,

probably in blue with a clearly visible white edge. It bears the crossed hammer and wrench beneath the coat of arms of the USSR. It is quite similar in shape to the academy badges worn by the police officer sitting at the left end of the table. Note the bust of Lenin, paintings of Marx and Engels, and the Red Flag.

(Right) Railway High School students' cap badge, 1984. This badge is similar to that of other technical schools (see page 142), but identified by the crossed hammer and wrench as specifically that of a railway institution.

(Right) Some rare collar patch emblems, mid-1970s. (Left to right): mine rescue workers; mine instructors and inspectors; telegraphists.

(Left) Telegraphist of the Ministry of Telecommunications, 1949. The uniform has the pre-1942 fall collar with piping around the edges, and piped cuffs, worn by officer-equivalent senior personnel. Note the attributes of telegraph and postal staff: stars as rank indicators, hammer-and-sickle buttons, and left sleeve patch with hammer, sickle and lightning flash (later this also appeared on collar patches - see previous picture).

(Below left) Ambulance driver's sleeve patch. The legend reads 'First Aid, Leningrad'; '03' is the telephone number of the ambulance service.

(Below) Ambulance driver's sleeve patch. This example is from a children's hospital, probably in Leningrad. The legend reads 'Children's Diagnostic Centre, Riverside Medical District'.

(Above) Miner, c.1953. It is hard to tell for what occasions this uniform was used. It is neither parade dress, nor working clothing - since it is white; perhaps it was used by administrative and transport personnel and students. It is easy to identify him as a miner, however, by the shape of the crossed hammers on his collar patches.

(Above) Miners, mid-1930s. Red Army engineer cadets during a period of practical training, photographed at the entrance to a coalmine in c.1935. Note the cropped heads and new, badly-fitting work clothes. Only one man (fifth from right, foreground) has a protective helmet. The waterproof hood (right, foreground) was still in use by the Soviet Army in the 1970s (see Book 1 page 85).

(Right) Mining academy student, 1954. This mine engineering student at the Ministry of Higher Education's Lvov Polytechnic Institute has the double-breasted miners' parade uniform with Gorny Institut (Mine and Mountain Institute, 'GI') shoulderboards. There are two different shapes of crossed miners' hammers on the collar patches and the buttons. A cap was also used with the same hammers badge. The parade uniform was worn with various - but always striped - shirts and ties. From 1955, when the Army was undergoing its uniform reforms, the miners' collar patches were removed, the collar buttons became smaller, and the notch between collar and lapel became horizontal. Note his Komsomol badge - and his hairstyle, typical of the period.

(Far left) Miners' cap badge, 1977. This version was used by all categories of engineering and technical workers. Various specialist mining personnel (eg. ventilation, electrical, mechanical, transport, command) had different cap badges, especially in the 1950s. Rank was sometimes indicated with stars above the badge, of the same pattern as worn on shoulderboards.

(Left) Ministry of Geology sleeve patch, early 1980s. This was used by engineers searching for non-renewable natural resources such as coal, oil, gas, diamonds, gold, iron, uranium, etc.

(Above left and right) Ministry of Geology Special Rescue Team sleeve patches. This militarised team was called in to help in cases of deep mine disasters or earthquakes. The two patches are earlier and later versions from the 1970s and early 1990s respectively. In 1953 they received their own uniform for the first time, including a visored cap; the cap badge at that time was a red star with crossed hammers and a gas mask.

(Far left) Professional Technical Schools cap badge. This badge was worn by students from 1968.

(Left) Medal 'Glory of the Miners' 3rd Class, c.1970s-80s.

Miscellaneous Collectibles

O ne approach related to militaria collecting is to hunt down parts of military vehicles, especially armoured vehicles, boats and aircraft. Since a complete and functioning T-34 or MiG-21 are too expensive and space-consuming for all but the wealthiest collectors, for most of us it is enough to acquire significant parts from them.

(Below) Gauges from the GAZ-69 vehicle. (Left to right): gasoline/petrol, battery charge, water temperature. The codes for companies building military vehicles were as follows:
UAZ: *Ulyanovsk (Lenin's birthplace in Siberia) Car Factory; mostly command vehicles.*
GAZ: *Gorky Car Factory; mostly trucks.*
VAZ: *River Volga Car Company, in the city named after Togliatti, the Italian Communist hero; Lada and Niva cars, mostly for Militia.*
ZIS: *Company named after Stalin, in Moscow; commanders' and diplomats' parade cars.*
ZIL: *The ZIS company renamed after Lihatsev; mostly trucks.*
Latvija: *In the 'Balticum'; small mil-* *itary vans, ambulances, minibuses, etc.*

(Bottom) It pleases some collectors to find new uses for parts taken from large pieces of military equipment, like these gauges from aircraft control panels. For example, the working manoeuvre watch (left) could make a nice table watch; it shows the time and the duration of the flight, and has a chronograph function. It might be harder to devise a new function for the bomb release control mechanism (centre) linked to the minimum altitude of the plane.

(Right) The humblest of souvenirs of the old USSR, but not without its poignancy: a gasoline token from the 1950s, valid for 5 litres of tractor fuel.

(Below) Altogether more desirable items are cameras. This FED model was produced from 1934 as a licensed version of the German Leica. It was named after Felix Dzerzhinsky, the head of the original Cheka state security service. After the 1917 Revolution and consequent Civil War one of the most pressing social problems was the huge number of young homeless trying to survive on the streets and in the countryside in times of famine and disorder. Inevitably, many turned to crime; hundreds of thousands of so-called bezprizorniks were frightening the citizens, especially in the Ukraine. The Soviet state security authorities organised no fewer than 550 rehabilitation camps for them. The first was the Gorky Settlement (1920); the best-known was the Dzerzhinsky Commune (1928), where this camera was produced by the youngsters as a part of the 'work therapy' based on the methods of a Ukrainian teacher named Makarenko.

(Right) The Moscow 4 camera was produced from 1945, following the latest German technical ideas of the Zeiss company's Ikonta model. A part of that company's machines and know-how were taken back to the USSR after the war as reparations. Note the hand-made wooden film spools.